Under the Chinaberry Tree

East Texas Folkways

Tumbleweed Smith

EAKIN PRESS ✦ Austin, Texas

Photos courtesy of
Rick Vanderpool
PRAIRIE ROSE STUDIO
Commerce, Texas
unless otherwise noted

FIRST EDITION
Copyright © 2002
By Tumbleweed Smith
Published in the United States of America
By Eakin Press
A Division of Sunbelt Media, Inc.
P.O. Drawer 90159 ⌨ Austin, Texas 78709-0159
email: sales@eakinpress.com
🖳 website: www.eakinpress.com 🖳
ALL RIGHTS RESERVED.
1   2   3   4   5   6   7   8   9
1-57168-523-5

Library of Congress Cataloging-in-Publication Data
Smith, Tumbleweed.
    Under the chinaberry tree: a study of East Texas folkways / by
Tumbleweed Smith.– 1st ed.
        p.   cm.
    Includes bibliographical references.
    ISBN 1-57168-523-5 (PB : alk. paper)
    1. Texas, East—Social life and customs—Anecdotes. 2. Texas,
East—History—Anecdotes.   3. Folklore—Texas, East—
Anecdotes. I. Title
F386.6 .S65   2002
976.4'2–dc21   2002005108

Contents

Preface

East Texas trademarks are water and trees. If it doesn't have water and trees, it's not East Texas. East Texans worship water and trees. Their lives revolve around a well, spring, branch, stream, bayou, pond, brook, creek, river, or lake. And they love to live in the woods.

Trees, like water, give them security. The trees also give them squirrels. East Texans love to hunt squirrels.

My parents, grandparents, cousins, aunts, and uncles lived in East Texas. I spent a good portion of my youth going barefoot down sandy lanes, fishing in swamps, and squirrel hunting in the woods behind Aunt Hattie's house.

The bed I slept on had a homemade feather mattress and was on a screened-in porch. Sometimes I helped my mother and her sisters shell peas under a chinaberry tree with a fat trunk and dark green leaves. The hard-packed ground around the tree was swept clean with a leafy chinaberry branch to keep the snakes away. I bathed in a washtub filled with water heated on a wood burning stove. I'm not that old. It's just that modern times were slow in getting to parts of rural East Texas.

East Texas is a red clay road underneath an umbrella of trees. The roadway is dark because no sun can pass through.

East Texas is history. Texas began in East Texas. For a long time, East Texas was all of Texas. It is the place to which the first settlers came.

It's Old Bethel and Tundra and Ben Wheeler and Athens and Canton.

It's dogwood coming to life in the spring, filling the woods with what appears to be bright popcorn. Magnolias, gum trees, Spanish moss, and wisteria decorate the countryside.

East Texas has its own distinctive sounds: A crow calls across a valley on a foggy morning. A squirrel chatters. The trees muffle the sounds as they ripple through the woods.

When the sun rises high in April, East Texas becomes a land adorned with flaming colors. A fish jumps in a spring-fed lake, its crystal clear water reflecting a wooded hillside and a blue sky.

My memories of East Texas are rural: mules, overalls, sunbonnets, gourd dippers, churns, coal oil lamps, and outhouses. Town was Duke & Ayres Five and Dime, the cattle auction barn, the hardware store, and church.

East Texas is a land of milk and honey. And nuts and flowers and birds and berries. Where people are friendly and sincere.

East Texas pioneers were determined to make a home and forego security for opportunity. They were experts at survival and had deep feelings for the region. So they set about building East Texas into what it is today.

They turned the diverse natural resources into monuments of pride and devotion.

The dreamers came and developed the cotton, the timber, the coal, the oil, the iron; they transformed the black land and red clay into dynamic cities while retaining the tranquility of the country.

East Texans emphasize family, work, and prayer—anchors in changing times and changing attitudes.

East Texas is a beautiful place.

Defining the Boundaries

When you start dividing Texas into different areas, some people get their feelings hurt and disagree with the boundary lines. When it comes to East Texas, though, residents don't pay much attention to where some writer draws a line on the map. They think the whole process is nutty, anyway. They know they live in East Texas and they don't want to move.

Most of them will agree that Tyler and Nacogdoches are in deep East Texas. Now, Athens is a different story. It's barely east of Interstate 45. And recently a whole lot of Metroplex folks have been buying property around Athens and attending the fiddlers' contest and black-eyed pea jamboree on the Henderson County courthouse lawn. They've been soaking up local color while sticking out like a sore thumb.

Canton used to be considered East Texas until First Monday started drawing such a crowd of Dallas folks that Canton lost much of its charm and character, the things that made visitors want to go there in the first place.

Are Dallas and Houston in East Texas? Both are too big to be considered belonging to any single part of the state. They are entities and geographic areas unto themselves. They happen to be in Texas and are just like any other big cities anywhere in the world. In other words, Dallas and Houston are not very interesting to someone who's looking for the real Texas spirit and flavor.

Corsicana is a good deal south of Dallas, but is still close enough to be influenced by the big city. Besides, Corsicana has more of a Central Texas feel to it and residents there identify with areas to the south and west.

The western boundary of East Texas starts about Quinlan, winds down to Terrell and Kaufman and Ennis, then roughly follows Interstate 45 down to New Waverly south of Huntsville. The southern boundary of East Texas stretches from New Waverly to the Sabine River, following along the line that links the cities of Evergreen, Coldspring, Wildwood, and Bon Weir.

The eastern boundary of East Texas follows the Sabine River from Bon Weir up to Caddo Lake. The northern boundary includes the cities of Jefferson, Gilmer, Emory, and Quinlan.

The Big Thicket, although considered to be part of East Texas, is mostly in Southeast Texas, an area that has a pull to the Gulf of Mexico. Likewise,

Northeast Texas is distinguished by its lack of pine trees. For a place to be in real East Texas, it has to have pine trees.

The coastal prairie defines the southeastern corner of East Texas, and the blackland prairie is along the northern border of the region.

So we have defined our focus. We might occasionally stray outside the defined borders for a story or two, but mostly we're looking at people, places, and events in East Texas, a part of the world that made our state famous.

Photo taken by Tumbleweed Smith

Texas: An Overview

In the last 300 years or so, some colorful characters have helped to develop Texas into what it is today. These characters include Indians, adventurers, missionaries, cowboys, cattle kings, homesteaders, cotton planters, miners, lumberjacks, and oil drillers.

The flags of six nations—Spain, France, Mexico, the Republic of Texas, the Confederate States, and the United States—have flown over Texas.

The western border of Texas is closer to the Pacific than to Port Arthur. The eastern boundary is closer to the Atlantic than it is to El Paso.

Texas produces more oil, beef cattle, sheep, goats, horses, cotton, and rice than any other state.

Most of the rain in Texas falls in East Texas. The Brazos River flows through rich farmland. The Sabine River carries great quantities of logs to sawmills.

Forests cover about 27 million acres of land, or about 16 percent of Texas. More than 120 types of trees grow in Texas, including pines, oaks, walnut, and gum.

More than 4,000 types of wildflowers grow in Texas.

The First Texans

Indians possessed the land of Texas for perhaps ten thousand years before the first European influences reached America through Columbus and his followers. The Indians of Texas are descendants of people that crossed over from Asia on the Bering Straits. Some stopped along the way; others pushed on southward. North, Central, and South America were peopled by their offspring.

The Gulf Coast tribes of Texas were fish and shell food eaters while the eastern Texas woodlands people were agriculturists.

Among the tribes indigenous to Texas were the Karankawa on the Gulf coast, the Tonkawa between the Colorado and Trinity rivers in the eastern central section, the Bidai and the Orocoquiza on the lower Trinity River, the Attacapa on the lower Neches and Sabine rivers, the Caddo and related tribes on the Red, Sabine, Neches, Trinity, Brazos, and Colorado rivers; and the Hasinai, Nacogdoche, Nabedache, and Anadarko in the valleys of the upper Neches and Angelina rivers.

The intrusive tribes in Texas included two groups: (1) those which were forced into Texas by the pressure of hostile tribes (chiefly Sioux) to the north and (2) those which were forced into Texas by pressure of white settlement from the east.

The vast woodlands of eastern Texas formed the refuge of tribes forced eastward because of colonial expansion following the American Revolution and the War of 1812. Chief among these tribes were the Choctaw and Chickasaw from Mississippi and Georgia, who settled on the Wichita, Sabine, and Neches rivers, and on the Red River near the Caddo; the Alabama-Coushatta from Alabama, who settled on the Sabine and Trinity rivers and who remained in Texas; the Kickapoo and Potawatomi from Illinois, who settled along the headwaters of the Sabine and Trinity rivers; the Delaware and Shawnee, who migrated from Missouri and found a Texas home south of the Red River near Pecan Point; the Quapaw, who came from their home on the Arkansas and White rivers to settle south of Red River on Sulphur Creek; a small group of the Creek from Alabama or Georgia, who established themselves in East Texas; and the final and most important of the migrant groups from the East, the Cherokee, who came from the Southern Appalachian Mountain region and settled in the Caddo territory south of the Red River, occupying land along the Angelina, Neches, and Sabine rivers.

When Columbus discovered America, he took back to Spain some Indians adorned with gold ornaments. The word spread over Europe that America was a rich country, much richer than Spain. When Spanish explorers began to search the seas for new, rich countries, they found gold mines in Central and South America. They concentrated on the land from Mexico southward, not paying much attention to Texas.

The Texas coast was first mapped in 1519 by Spanish sea captain Álvarez de Pineda. Nine years later, in November of 1528, Alvar Núñez Cabeza de Vaca and three other members of the Pánfilo de Narváez expedition were shipwrecked on an island near present-day Galveston. It took seven years for the survivors to reach a Spanish settlement.

Their journey with various Indian tribes was remarkable.

De Vaca's tales of Indian legends about seven cities of

gold aroused enough interest for the Spanish viceroy to send Francisco Vásquez de Coronado on an expedition through the high plains. The first real effort to establish missions among Indians came with Coronado. A few missions were built, but no permanent development resulted from the expeditions between the Mississippi and Brazos rivers. Spanish efforts to settle Texas were not renewed until French activity east of the region began in 1685.

France began exploring America in 1685, when Robert Cavelier, Sieur de la Salle, who had claimed Louisiana for France in 1682, was washed ashore by a storm at Matagorda Bay. La Salle founded a place called Fort Saint Louis several miles inland near present-day Woodville. He made several forays into the West seeking gold and silver. One of his men killed him in 1687 after a quarrel at a site near Navasota. That city now has a monument to La Salle at a spot thought to be his burial place. Disease and Indians killed off the white men and destroyed Fort Saint Louis.

The Spaniards were alarmed at La Salle's explorations, and in 1689 an expedition led by Ponce de León set out from Mexico to destroy Fort Saint Louis. When they found the ruins, they continued eastward. In 1690 a missionary with de León's expedition established the first mission, San Francisco de los Tejas, in East Texas. It stood near the present-day city of Weches.

Spain's method of conquering the New World was completely dependent on finding available savages to Christianize and Hispanicize. The aim of church and state, then synonymous in Spain, was to create agricultural Indian societies. The early missions were fully an agency of the state, and the missionary priests were agents of the Crown, which subsidized them and provided the necessary military protection.

The Crown would receive its own reward when the natives became hard-working, tax-paying citizens, subject to military service and other duties, and with about the same privileges and status as the peasants of Old Spain.

The Spanish put more attention, money, and effort into their system than any contemporary European power, but the Spaniards had never before come across a breed of people like those they found in Texas—people who would not be conquered.

The Caddo Indians had many villages in the vicinity where they lived in relative comfort, planting vegetables and corn in the spring while hunting and fishing in the rich region in other seasons. Members of the largest tribe in Texas lived a secure, leisurely life.

The Caddoans were the most civilized tribe of Texas Indians and therefore held the most promise of quick Hispanicization. But they refused to adopt Christianity and Spanish serfdom.

Being unwarlike, the Caddos welcomed the Spaniards into their forest. They watched the priests dedicate the mission and celebrate the colorful Mass. The Indians were impressed with the pageantry. They listened gravely to the priests, presented the soldiers with corn and other foods, and promised to give thought to the matter of becoming mission Indians.

The Caddos were more amused than afraid of the idea of year-round work in the fields, and since they lived in a timeless world, they were in no hurry to make changes.

Spanish soldiers, far from home for a long period of time, began to teach the Indian girls about things other than the Christian faith. This put the visitors from Spain in a bad light.

Then the Spaniards unintentionally transmitted a lethal epidemic to the tribe. What the Europeans called normal childhood diseases, such as measles, were fatal pestilences to all Texas Indians. The Caddos were decimated. Survivors avoided the mission.

Since the mission was dependent on the natives for food, it went into decline. By 1692 the mission of San Francisco de los Tejas was abandoned and the Spaniards marched back to Mexico.

The adoption of the name of Texas for the area came during this time. An Indian was asked the name of his tribe and he replied "Tejas," from

the Caddoan word "Teychas" meaning allies or friends. This word was spelled "Texas" frequently in old Spanish, in which the "x" was substituted for a "j" sound. The Spaniards began to use the name to refer to the land between the Rio Grande and the Red River, and it is known today as Texas.

In 1713 the Sieur de Cadillac, governor of the new province of Louisiana, sent the Canadian explorer St. Denis up the river to build a fort on Spanish soil. France's claims to Texas had never been fully relinquished.

The French were more interested in trade than territory; they were not much concerned with converting or incorporat-

ing the natives, or pushing them off their land. Thus their aim and approach were entirely different from the Spaniards in America.

The French were successful in getting along with the Indians, since their approach neither enslaved nor displaced the natives. The French also had the tendency to blend into the forests and even adopt much of the Indian way of life. They became the greatest traders, trappers, and squaw men of them all. Unlike other Europeans, the French sold the Indians guns, so their influence over most tribes became great.

In 1716 St. Denis, his wife, his father-in-law, and a large party of priests and soldiers marched into Texas to found four new mission-forts, including one at Nacogdoches. St. Denis became a popular figure on the frontier and directly caused the King of Spain to found a number of Texas forts and missions. Nuestra Señora de Guadalupe was established at the present site of Nacogdoches, and the Mission Nuestra Señora de los Dolores was placed near the site of present-day San Augustine.

This era of mission building marks the beginning of Texas statehood. It was officially declared a Spanish dominion and Domingo Terán de los Ríos was named governor in 1691. Political authority was relaxed and little attention was given Texas until the administration of Martin de Alarcon, governor of Coahuila-Texas, who founded the mission San Antonio de Valero and the presidio of San Antonio de Bexar in 1718. The mission had a chapel attached to it called the Alamo, a Spanish word for cottonwood.

In 1720 four missions—San José de Aguayo, La Purísima Concepcíon de Acuña, San Juan Capistrano, and San Francisco de la Espada—were rapidly founded in the San Antonio area. Three of them were re-establishments of the abandoned East Texas missions.

By 1731, Spain had sent more than ninety expeditions into Texas and established missions throughout the region. In 1772 San Antonio became the seat of Spanish government in Texas.

When the East Texas missions were abandoned a second time in 1776, the white population was removed to San Antonio. A number of these settlers returned under the leadership of Antonio Gil Ybarbo and settled around old mission Guadalupe near Nacogdoches in 1779.

The purposes of the missions were to Christianize the Indian, to extend frontiers of Spanish dominion, and to aid in establishing civil law. The missionaries also introduced European animals, and European agricultural implements and practices. The culture of their homeland began the nucleus of culture which attracted Anglo settlers.

In 1806 the only towns in Texas were San Antonio (2,000), Goliad (1,400), and Nacogdoches with nearly 500 residents. In spite of the constant dangers, many excellent American families settled near Nacogdoches. These settlers, with officers in the Mexican army, formed the higher circles of society. In San Antonio many settlers were descendants of aristocratic Spanish families. The army officers were generally men of polished manners. The priests were men of learning and refinement.

Mexico gained independence from Spain in 1821, and Texas became part of the Republic of Mexico. Despite a century of effort, Spain had made little headway in populating Texas. A buffer between the Indians and the Spanish settlement was needed.

In 1820 Moses Austin, a Missouri banker, traveled to San Antonio and asked Spanish officials to let him establish a colony of Americans in Texas. The Spanish government granted his request, but Austin died before he could organize the colony.

His son, Stephen F. Austin, carried out the plan and established 300 families in Texas. Stephen, college educated and practicing law in New Orleans, made an agreement with Spain for colonization of Texas in 1821. Mexico's independence forced him to visit Mexico City to get the grant reaffirmed by the new government. His colony of 300 families was camped on the Brazos. More than 1,000 land titles were issued to Austin in the next decade, and his colony grew to over 5,000.

In 1821 Austin and his group made its first settlements at Columbus and Washington-on-the-Brazos. His colony extended from the Gulf Coast to Central Texas and included

parts of the present-day counties of Bastrop, Burleson, and Lee. Austin's first settlers were called the "Old Three Hundred." Most of them came as farmers from the United States, but a substantial number arrived as men of means from the British Isles. All but four were educated. The most common home states were Louisiana, Alabama, Arkansas, Tennessee, and Missouri. The vast majority migrated to Texas for the chance to get cheap land. Most brought some form of capital: seeds, equipment, stock, or slaves.

Other colonies were fairly successful. Henri Castro brought 600 families to Castroville. W. S. Peters is credited with the settlement of families around present-day Dallas.

Hayden Edwards settled 800 families around Nacogdoches. There were already a good many Spanish-speaking people in the area who had lived on the lands for many years but who had no legal title to their farms. Some Americans had settled there, too, before Edwards received his contract.

Nearby were the Cherokee Indians, occupying lands within Edwards' grant. In such a situation, trouble was bound to develop. After some bickering, Edwards unwisely made an alliance with the Cherokees and declared Texas independent under the name of "Fredonia." He proposed to divide the land between his followers and the Cherokees. None of the Americans who were building their homes in the other colonies wanted to go to war with Mexico, and men of Austin's colony aided the Mexican authorities in putting down a small rebellion.

The skirmish made the Mexican government suspicious of the loyalty of the Americans in Texas. From that time on, in spite of the willingness of most of the settlers to live peaceably under Mexican rule, troubles multiplied.

Between 1821 and 1836, Texas' white population grew to between 30,000 and 35,000. Mexican officials became alarmed at the increasing numbers of American settlers. In the 1830s they halted Anglo-American settlement in Texas, and relations between the Texans and the Mexicans went into a decline.

A political convention was held at San Felipe de Austin on October 18, 1832. Such conventions were the ordinary American method of presenting complaints to their government, but the Mexicans knew nothing of such procedure.

Stephen F. Austin was elected chairman to, among other things, seek the right to use the English language in public business, to organize a militia, and to separate Texas from the Mexican state of Coahuila. When Austin carried the new constitution and petition for reforms to Mexico City, he was arrested. While detained in the Mexican capital, Austin sent word to the Texans to speed up their efforts to organize a state separate from Coahuila.

When General Antonio López de Santa Anna became president of Mexico in 1833, he immediately began making plans to become dictator of the country. He had been in office less than a year when he abolished the state governments and forced out of office all men who did not promise to aid him in his dictatorship. One after another the states of Mexico fell under his control, until only Zacatecas and Coahuila offered resistance. Determined to crush those who disputed his authority, the dictator sent armies to crush Zacatecas and Coahuila. In Texas the garrison at San Antonio had been strengthened, and General Martín Perfecto de Cos, brother-in-law of Santa Anna and commander of northern Mexico, was instructed first to crush the rebellion in Coahuila, then to establish himself at San Antonio to deal with the Texans.

When Santa Anna sent a company of soldiers to Anahuac to collect duties in 1835, colonists led by William Barret Travis forced the Mexicans to leave for San Antonio. General Cos ordered the arrest of Travis and others. When Austin returned from Mexico City, he announced that war was Texas' only recourse.

The Battle of Gonzales is usually considered the first battle of the Texas Revolution. Gonzales settlers had a cannon, which had been placed there years before to protect the town against Indians. The commandant at San Antonio demanded the surrender of the cannon, but the men of Gonzales refused to give it up. A company of Mexican soldiers was then sent to get the cannon. On the morning of October 2, 1835, 160 Texans, armed with their rifles, marched against the Mexican camp. They had the cannon with them, and across it was draped a small sign which read "Come and Take It!" One Mexican was killed and one Texan wounded in the resulting battle. The cannon remained at Gonzales. The war of Texas Independence had started.

A week later, General Cos led his well-equipped army into San Antonio. He had left at Goliad thousands of dollars' worth of Mexican military supplies and munitions, which the Texans seized. All through the settlements, word spread that General Cos and his troops were in San Antonio. The Texans organized an army of men without uniforms or military experience, but who could "shoot straight and keep their powder dry." They proposed to defeat the best-equipped and largest military force that had ever visited Texas. On December 8 they reached the heart of San Antonio and forced General Cos into the Alamo, where he surrendered. He marched 1,100 of his men back to Mexico. When Cos' army crossed the Rio Grande on Christmas Day, not a Mexican soldier remained on the soil of Texas.

The Texans knew that Santa Anna would certainly attempt to punish them for the humiliation suffered by Cos' soldiers. Santa Anna had been victorious in every other part of Mexico. He would come personally to Texas at the head of a great army to force the colonists to submit to his dictatorship or to flee beyond the Sabine River. The Texans decided to fight for their rights.

A constitutional convention was held at Washington-on-the-Brazos, a modest community of cabins and shanties. The delegates met in an unfinished carpenter shop, which had no doors or windows. A norther swept down as the meeting opened. On March 2, 1836, the Texas Declaration of Independence was adopted by a unanimous vote. The Texans declared themselves free of Mexico and elected an interim government until an official election could be held. David Burnet was named president of the Republic of Texas, Lorenzo de Zavala was named vice president, and Sam Houston was named commander in chief of the military.

During the convention, Santa Anna was completing his journey to Texas. He was in San Antonio with 6,000 troops. On March 2, the very day that Texas became free of Mexico, Santa Anna took charge of the assault on the Alamo, where a band of Texas soldiers was fighting against over-whelming odds. William B. Travis, James Bowie, David Crockett, and others were determined to hold the Alamo, even if it cost them their lives. They cried out, "We consider death preferable to disgrace."

At dawn on March 6 the Battle of the Alamo was over.

News of the disaster spread panic throughout the settlements. The Convention at Washington-on-the-Brazos finished its business, and members hurried off to protect their families. Some settlers gathered their families and headed toward the safety of the United States, just beyond the Sabine River. The flight of the settlers was referred to as the Runaway Scrape.

One division of the Mexican army under General Urrea marched up from Matamoros, annihilating detachments of the Texas army as it headed north. It surrounded Colonel Fannin's command near Goliad. After a desperate fight, the Texans surrendered on March 20 and returned to Goliad as prisoners of the Mexicans. There, at daybreak on March 27, they were marched out in squads and shot down by order of Santa Anna.

The events at the Alamo and at Goliad formed a battle cry for the showdown battle at San Jacinto: "Remember the Alamo! Remember Goliad!"

Santa Anna thought the Alamo and Goliad massacres had broken the resistance of the Texans. He scattered his troops widely for the purpose of exterminating the Texan soldiers that remained. On April 20, 1,150 troops under Santa Anna's personal command found themselves face to face with the Texans at Buffalo Bayou. The remainder of the Mexican army was scattered miles away.

On April 21, at San Jacinto, Santa Anna and his troops decided to take a siesta. Strangely enough, both the Texans and Mexicans had decided not to attack until the following day. But some Texan soldiers, who had not yet learned military discipline, set aside the decision of their officers and attacked the resting Mexicans that afternoon. The Mexicans

were taken completely by surprise. The Texans charged through the camp like madmen, shouting, "Remember the Alamo! Remember Goliad!" Santa Anna was awakened by the shouting and the shooting and soon found himself crawling through the tall grass in an effort to save his life. The battle was over in less than twenty minutes. The war was over, and Texas was an independent nation.

The Republic of Texas lasted nine years. Its white population was only about 30,000 when it declared its independence, and hardly more than 100,000 in 1845 when Texas became a state. Texas didn't do too well as a new republic. Its treasury was empty, and raiding Indians and Mexicans threatened its people. Voters elected Sam Houston president and wanted him to seek annexation to the U.S.

A serious disturbance broke out in East Texas in 1842 over charges of land fraud. Shelby County, which then included a large portion of East Texas, became two armed camps known as the Regulators and Moderators. Over a two-year period, some fifty men were slain and courts ceased to function. The disturbance was stopped in 1844, but bitterness lasted for many years.

Texans voted in favor of annexation in 1836, but opposition to slavery delayed acceptance until 1845.

The statehood ceremony took place in front of the log cabin that had served as the capitol of the Republic. Nothing quite like this is recorded in history. A free and independent republic was voluntarily giving up its sovereignty in order to become a part of another nation. President Anson Jones, the last president of the Republic of Texas, delivered his final official address to the gathered crowd: "The great measure of annexation, so earnestly desired by the people of Texas, is happily consummated. The Lone Star of Texas, which ten years ago rose amid clouds over fields of carnage and obscurely shone for awhile, has become fixed in that glorious constellation, the American Union. The final act of this great drama is now performed. The Republic of Texas is no more."

After Texas was annexed to the U.S., Mexico broke off diplomatic relations with the U.S. Disputes arose over the boundary between Texas and Mexico. The Mexican War followed in 1846. In the 1848 Treaty of Guadalupe Hidalgo, which ended the war, Mexico gave up all claim to Texas and established the Rio Grande as the boundary between the two countries.

Settlers, chased off by the war, flocked back to the state, and by 1850 the population had grown to 213,000. By 1860, about 600,000 people lived in Texas, most of them in the country. The state had seventy-one newspapers with a total circulation of 100,000. Ninety-five percent of the white population could read, and some publication reached virtually every family.

Sam Houston became the first United States senator from Texas. Indian troubles were still a hindrance to outlying stretches of the state when the rumblings of slavery and secession descended on the South. The vast majority of Texans sympathized with the people of the Old South, whose customs had become a part of the new state and huge plantations had their quota of slaves. The question shook the foundations of the state government. Sam Houston was opposed to secession from the Union, but the majority of delegates to a convention in January of 1861 voted to side with the Confederacy. On March 16 the convention declared the office of governor vacant, and the Constitution of the Confederacy was ratified on March 23. Within a month Texas had furnished 8,000 men for the Confederate army.

Few major Civil War battles were fought in Texas, but the final battle of the war was fought in the state. At Palmito Ranch near Brownsville on May 13, 1865, Colonel Ford defeated 800 Federal troops and to his surprise learned that Robert E. Lee had surrendered on April 9, more than a month earlier.

Texas suffered little during the war. It was the only Confederate state that was not overrun by the invaders. Good crops were harvested every year and business never wavered in its growth. The Union troops were never able to stop Texas trade across the Rio Grande. At the end of the war, Texas had more money and foodstuffs than all the rest of the South put together.

After the Civil War, Northern sympathizers rose to power in Texas politics. Race riots flared, and the Ku Klux Klan became powerful. From 1865 to 1869 the U.S. ruled Texas under a military government. Texas was re-admitted to the Union on March 30, 1870, when the state had more than 800,000 residents.

Around the House

Early settlers in East Texas were survivors. They had to be on the lookout for Indians or other raiding parties. Families tended to stay together, with members hardly getting out of

eyesight of each other. Their houses were small and cozy, and there was a strong sense of family closeness.

Most houses in early East Texas were made of wood. The outside walls were one-by-twelve planks with one-by-fours nailed over the seams where the one-by-twelves came together. The houses were built on piers and beams. Items like hoses, tubs, and even an occasional box springs were usually stored under the house.

Every home had a shotgun. It was used to chase off would-be predators, whether they walked on two feet or four. It was also used to hunt squirrels. And when ammunition ran low, some enterprising hunters caught squirrels by hitting them with rocks or sticks.

Hunting is an East Texas tradition. It has always been a contest that pits the skills of man against the instincts of animals. In the early days, men liked to see how close they could get to an animal or bird without being seen. Since there was plenty of time, men became experts at the hunt and made a science out of it.

Once they got the squirrel, they used all of it. The skin was used to make hats or coats. Some people even cut around the outside of the hide and made shoestrings. The meat was used to make stew or was eaten fried or baked.

On a hunt, generally the hunters were quiet. They listened for the slightest sound that might indicate where some game might be.

The East Texas woods are filled with pigs, deer, squirrel, raccoon, possum, birds, and other things that are good to eat. Streams are filled with fish, and berries grow on bushes. Nut trees helped the early pioneers, too.

In fact, if an East Texas family settled down in the woods, about the only things they needed from a store were coffee, flour, and sugar. Syrup came from the cane mills. Milk came from a cow. Water came from either a spring or a shallow well.

Transportation was no problem. There wasn't much need for it anyway. A wagon did just fine. Just hitch the horse or mule to it and take off.

Iced tea was always drunk from a fruit jar. Meals were eaten on an oilcloth. The kids sat on benches and the parents sat in chairs at either end of the table. Silverware was kept in a jar in the middle of the table.

A number-three washtub was used for bathing. Water was heated on a wood-burning stove. People slept on mattresses filled with down feathers gathered from the chests of geese. Some of those mattresses have lasted five generations.

If you went to the little store within walking distance, candy was mostly peanut patties. They were unwrapped, and the wooden box they were in was covered with a moist cloth.

Gallon jars of milk were kept cool by submerging them in the spring. The clear, clean water wasn't to be disturbed when you put the jar in or took it out. Country folks are very protective of their water supply.

They honored their dead by cleaning the cemeteries. Once a year they met and worked all day getting weeds and other undesirable things from around the gravesites. They paused long enough in the middle of the day for a lavish meal.

Most every home had a storm cellar. The soil was easy to dig. It was either sand or clay, with few rocks. The cellar was used primarily to store items that had been canned. Most of the time they were wonderful, mysterious places for youngsters to explore. But sometimes cellars were scary. Sometimes kids found snakes in them, sending the youngsters back outside into the safety of open air.

The barn was an adventure for youngsters, too. Most people picture barns as large structures. But not all barns are big. The bigger a barn is, the more money it costs. Back when barns were first being built, East Texans generally were poor, so some barns were the size of a bedroom.

You usually could find something to eat in an East Texas barn. Especially peanuts. Some farmers kept a toesack full of freshly picked peanuts by the door. The peanuts still had the stems on them. The barn also held bridles, saddles, and other tack items for horses, bales of hay, and old discarded tools and furniture.

Lye soap was on the washstand by the back door and was used to wash hands, dishes, and clothes. Water was heated in a big black pot, and the clothes were punched with a big stick while they were soaking in the near boiling water.

The pot had to be emptied and filled several times for each washing and rinsing. Then the clothes were hung out to dry on wires strung between posts. They were ironed with heavy irons that were heated on the wood stove.

The front porch swing was like a throne. Papa sat in it. Sometimes he would be joined by Mama. But the kids just sat on the porch. Papa smoked a pipe if he wanted to, and everybody talked about the day past and the one coming.

Porches were special places. Especially if they were screened to keep the little flying things away. Electricity wasn't all that necessary. A coal oil or kerosene lamp provided a nice glow.

Many rural areas of East Texas didn't get electricity until the '50s. Some people say electricity changed their lives, and not so much for the better. With electricity came speed, cars, and a whole set of new problems.

Tractors were the big things in farming. A single plow hitched to a mule or the farmer's wife was replaced by something that was big, noisy, and ran on gasoline. Things were changing, for sure.

It seemed as if some kind of maniac was always on the loose. Or maybe it was just the adults keeping the children charged up. Anyway, storytelling was a good pastime then, and most of the stories were scary.

Country boys went barefoot as soon as warm weather hit in early spring. By summer's end their feet were tough enough to run through a briar patch without getting anything stuck in them. The outer layer of skin had been hardened by months of pounding over sand, stickers, rocks, wooden steps, and the yard, which was nearly as hard as concrete.

The black pot was an important article in the East Texan's life. It was used for washing clothes and making things like lye soap. The black pot ordinarily stayed in one place, since it was too heavy and bulky to move around. The pot's handles were used primarily to empty the water or other liquids it held.

The black pots were sturdy vessels. They could sit on a fire for days and never wear out. The housewife used a big stick, either a tree branch or part of a broom handle, to poke the clothes in the pot on washday. When the clothes were washed, the pot was used for rinsing, then the clothes were hung on a clothes line to dry. The pot ordinarily stayed just a few feet from the water well to make carrying the water back and forth more convenient.

The water well was dug down into the East Texas sand, sometimes with a pick and shovel. Homeowners did the work themselves, even bricking up the sides. They usually built a rock well wall above the ground about four feet high and put a wooden top on it with a hinged square in the middle to provide easy access to the water. A pulley on a crossbar above the well held a bucket that was lowered down into the well by a rope.

The well was near the kitchen door of the house. Next to the door was a shelf containing a bucket of water, a gourd dipper for drinking, a wash basin, and a bar of soap. This served as an outdoor washroom where the husband and children could clean up before mealtimes. To get a cool drink from a gourd dipper during the heat of the day was a special treat.

Somewhere along the wall of the house, most likely on the back wall, a washtub hung on a nail, with the open side of the tub toward the house.

Away from the main house was the outhouse. A simple hole about eight feet deep was dug in the sand, and a crude, small structure was built over it. A bench-type seat was inside, with anywhere from one to four holes in it. Usually a catalogue of some sort, perhaps from Montgomery Ward or Sears, was either hung on a string or placed somewhere on the bench for easy access. These were referred to as "wishbooks."

Jefferson

Most East Texans identify with the South because most of them come from there. They migrated into Texas from Alabama or Mississippi, the area referred to as the "old country." Southern customs abound in East Texas.

Jefferson, in the northeast corner of East Texas, has a

number of antebellum homes, cobblestone streets, and ancient brick walls that show the influence of the South on architecture and city planning. Jefferson residents have a distinct southern accent.

Jefferson is truly unique. Some ladies, members of the Jessie Allen Wise garden club, have been busy for years restoring old homes. Under the guidance of Lucille Terry, the club made sure Jefferson stayed on the tourist map by continually adding new diversions for visitors. The city has ninety-two buildings with historic status.

Every spring the city has a tour of homes. It is during this time that the Diamond Bessie Murder Trial plays to packed houses. It is a courtroom drama based on a Jefferson murder which occurred in the 1890s. The Excelsior House hotel stays full, as do a number of bed-and-breakfast places. You can take a surrey ride around town, a boat trip along Big Cypress Bayou, or shop in Jefferson's stores for antiques.

Jefferson was once called "The Mother of Texas." It was the state's primary inland port, industrial city, and plantation center. In 1880 the population was 35,000, making it one of the largest cities in the state. It was the first town in Texas to have artificial gaslights and the first to manufacture ice. The first beer in Texas was brewed in Jefferson.

In 1882 railroad tycoon Jay Gould tried to convince the residents of Jefferson to let him bring his railroad through town. The town refused, saying railroads had an uncertain future and would never replace steamboats. Gould left in a huff, telling the people of Jefferson, "Grass will grow in your streets." He was nearly correct. He moved his operation to Marshall, his Texas and Pacific Railroad roared westward, and the steamboat era faded. Jefferson went into decline.

Today, Gould's private railroad car is a big tourist attraction. It sits across the street from the Excelsior House. People are amazed at the fine wood, heavy drapes, and sterling silver sink and bathtub. The railroad car was acquired some years ago after several migrant families had used it for a home.

Jefferson was a steamship town. It was settled in 1832 by a handful of Anglo-Americans who discovered a ferry operation seven miles east of Jefferson on Big Cypress Bayou, operated by S. P. Smith. There was a Caddo Indian village nearby, but as more settlers arrived, the Indians moved on.

Big Cypress was navigable water, connected through the Red River to the Mississippi. Early day shipping prospered, but defective land titles obstructed development at Smith's Landing.

Jefferson was established in 1836 on land donated by Allen Urquart, a ferry operator. It was on Trammel's Trace, over which Sam Houston and later David Crockett entered Texas. Large sawmills were erected in the nearby forests, and the town soon became the main river port in Texas. Paddle-wheel steamers from New Orleans and St. Louis regularly made stops in Jefferson. Oxcarts and wagons brought the produce of East Texas to Jefferson's wharves to be transported to other markets. Cotton from East Texas was loaded at Jefferson and shipped all over the world. As many as 226 steamboats a year docked in Jefferson in the 1800s, unloading goods from the East and onloading cargoes bound for New Orleans. Jefferson became a major port because of a freakish situation that existed in the Red River, some thirty miles to the east.

Untold centuries of uprooted trees, silt, moss, vines, and every other kind of debris had formed what amounted to a thick raft that served as an enormous water trap. This caused the stream level of the bayou tributary in Jefferson to stand ten feet above its ordinary height. When the U.S. Corps of Engineers began to remove the natural logjam, the water level receded and Jefferson's steamboat traffic passed into history.

The years of the Texas Republic, 1836 to 1845, saw a big immigrant rush from the Southern states. Many of them arrived by steamship at Jefferson.

Jefferson was laid out as a townsite in 1843, and in 1846 it became the seat of Cass County. When that county separated from Bowie County, the Cass County seat was moved to Linden in 1852.

In the early 1850s an iron foundry was established by Lockett and Stewart. A young foreman, George Addison Kelly, developed the Kelly plow, which was responsible for moving mountains of East Texas earth.

A destructive fire in Jefferson in 1866 caused a new waterfront to be built, and several new mercantile establishments were opened.

In 1867 artificial gas was made by subjecting pine knots to intense heat in iron drums or conical retorts. The gas issuing from the top of the cone was carried into mains laid under the principal streets, along which ornamental gaslight fixtures were installed.

In 1868 a man named Doyle devised a method of freezing water in thin, flat pans. Built up by layers and congealed into blocks, the ice was sold for ten cents a pound. The undertaking was not a success, but it paved the way for future ice-making operations.

Jefferson, named for Thomas Jefferson, became the county seat of Marion County in 1860. Unlike other county seats built around a square, Jefferson was built along the Big Cypress Creek, with the streets laid out at right angles to the water.

During the Civil War, a meat cannery and boot factory were built in Jefferson. Jefferson reached full development around 1870.

Materials and furnishings of many of the early homes in Jefferson were brought up the river from New Orleans, and those homes and their antique furnishings have continued to give charm to the town.

Removal of the big Red River raft in 1874 destroyed navigation on Big Cypress Bayou, and the city suffered a financial setback. There was some increase in population when oil was discovered around Jefferson in 1938, but the town never regained the stature it had during the steamboat days.

Jefferson, with its picturesque brick streets, remains one of the most unique cities in Texas. If you spend a weekend in this "Belle of the Bayou" it'll be like visiting a Texas time capsule.

The Excelsior House Hotel—the state's

longest continuously operating hotel—serves perhaps the best breakfast in the state. The menu includes buttery grits, smoked ham, scrambled eggs, and orange blossom honey-nut muffins.

Jefferson is the home of the first bed-and-breakfast in Texas. Now the city has a dozen of them, as well as a number of hotels and motels and fine eating establishments.

There's plenty to do in this city of 2,800 people. The city has an excursion train, a fabulous museum, and a candlelight Christmas tour of homes held the first weekend in December each year. Nearby lakes and forests accommodate visitors seeking recreational activities. Lake O' the Pines features a sandy beach area. Caddo Lake, the state's only natural lake, has trees dripping with Spanish moss.

Caddo Lake

Caddo Lake, in the northeastern part of East Texas, is one of the largest natural lakes in the South. Named for the Caddo Indians, legend says the lake was formed by an earthquake caused when a Caddo chief failed to obey the Great Spirit.

A more realistic reason for the lake's existence would be that it was formed from the big logjam on the Red River (the Red River Raft). Around 1900 the U.S. government destroyed the logjam and built a dam near Mooringsport, Louisiana, to form the present Caddo Lake.

The lake straddles the boundary between Texas and Louisiana. It is known for its giant cypress trees, with overhanging branches so thick with leaves and Spanish moss they create darkness even in the middle of the day.

When the lake was first created, it was known as Fairy Lake.

Shreveport, Louisiana, businessmen caused the raft to be destroyed after noticing Jefferson prospering as the head of navigation. This act pulled the plug on both Jefferson and Caddo Lake, leaving Jefferson high and dry. Caddo was reduced to a swamp.

Another legend says the chief had a vision and told his followers to move their village to higher ground to escape the wall of water that would sweep over the village site. The tribe moved to the present location of the Caddo State Park and was saved.

When oil was discovered in the lake area just after the turn of the century, oil companies found it difficult to work in the shallow water of the lake. They successfully lobbied to get a small dam built a short distance below Mooringsport, thus enabling barge and workboat traffic to travel on the lake.

Bald cypress trees are numerous on the lake. A cypress seed will take root only in damp ground and will grow only in water an inch or two deep. The cypress breaks of today clearly define the former ponds, channels, and creeks of the old Caddo Lake.

Harriet Potter, wife of the secretary of the navy of the

Republic of Texas Robert Potter, wrote about her first impression of her Caddo Lake home:

> A place more beautiful than Potter's Point it would be impossible to imagine. I never tired of admiring the scenery that lay about my new home. Our home stood upon a jutting promontory that rose into a hill set in the midst of one of the grandest timber belts in Texas. The level timber lands circled about it, while for more than two hundred feet, a steep bank overlooked the most romantically beautiful lake that I've ever beheld. For eight miles one could look across to the opposite shore over a great sheet of sparkling water that washed up into the white beaches below the cliff and sang a soft song that the spirits of the forests caught up and carried on unseen wings into the forest's depths and tangled music in the meshes of the lofty tree tops.

Steamboat navigation on Caddo ceased in 1873-74. The booming economy drained away with the waters of Caddo Lake. The thriving river commerce was gone forever. The great plantations around the lake, which had flourished with slave labor and cheap transportation to the eastern textile mills, were now abandoned. The Civil War reconstruction had also taken its toll. Money was scarce.

Caddo Lake was still a great provider of natural resources, with an abundance of fish, wildfowl, squirrel, rabbit, deer, and numerous other types of wild game. Chinquapins, black walnuts, hickory nuts, persimmons, muscadines, and wild grapes were harvested in the fall. Mayhaws, blackberries, dewberries, wild plums, Indian peaches, and other delights began to ripen in early summer and were turned into the greatest jellies, jams, and preserves that were ever spread on a hot biscuit. They also made good wine.

Folks living around the lake spent money for things like flour, salt, shot, gunpowder, fish hooks, and twine. Commercial hunting and fishing became viable ways to earn a living.

Commercial fish were buffalo and catfish, but game fish such as white perch (crappie) or black bass were popular and brought higher prices. All the fish were easy to catch and the supply seemed endless.

The paddlefish, known locally as the spoonbill catfish, were netted for their roe, which was rushed to eastern markets by railway in iced wooden kegs and sold at premium prices as caviar.

Since the lake had been lowered, it was possible to wade into the water a great distance. Local fishermen soon discovered the bottom of the lake was covered with large fresh mussels. When removed from their shells, they made a cheap bait for trotlines.

Caddo Indians had made beautiful ornaments from the mother-of-pearl lining of the shells. There was great excite-

ment when fishermen began finding real pearls inside the mussel shells.

Hundreds, perhaps thousands, of people joined in the search for freshwater pearls in Caddo Lake. The shallow water and sandy shoreline made an ideal habitat for pearl-bearing mussels.

Many gatherers worked on their hands and knees and looked like hogs rooting through the mud. They came to be called "pearl hogs." At the height of the pearl boom, fires from pearl camps could be seen for miles around the shores of the lake.

George Murata, a Japanese man who went to Caddo as a cook, became an expert on Caddo pearls. He acted as a broker, buying and selling them in quantity. Prices ranged from a few dollars to about $1,500 for the best ones, a small fortune in those days.

George made selling trips to both coasts and became so well known at Tiffany's in New York he was allowed to show his pearls over the counter to customers. George became a wealthy man and lived well on Caddo.

When the first dam was built on Caddo Lake, the deeper water put an end to the pearling industry.

But another type of treasure lay below the lake: black gold. An oil discovery brought fortune seekers by the trainload. Caddo Lake provided one of the first locations where oil was known to be under water. It was in Caddo Lake that the basic underwater drilling techniques so widely used all over the world today were first developed and used.

Howard Hughes got his start on Caddo by going from well to well carrying a drill bit in a tow sack, trying to persuade drillers to use his bit to drill through rock. The bit worked well, and he founded Hughes Tool Company and became the richest man in the world. His fortune derived from the rotary rock bit which got its start on Caddo Lake.

Beer Boats on Caddo Lake

Fred Dahmer is a naturalist. He lives in the community of Uncertain. His house is just a few yards from Caddo Lake. Fred has explored the lake and its legends—and the people who have contributed to the legends.

He knows about the beer boats.

"The story of the Caddo Lake bootleggers has been told thousands of times," says Fred, "but seldom do you hear about the beerleggers." They were poor and not socially accepted by the wealthy distillers of rotgut.

When Prohibition ended, Harrison County voted to stay dry. But nearby Marion County voted wet. "The law was interpreted to mean that you couldn't even transport beer into Harrison County except with a federal license, which was issued only to legal beer distributors," says Fred.

Now, all the old-timers knew exactly where the two counties' boundary line was: in the center of the channel of Big Cypress Bayou.

It was not long before the Marion County side had a pontoon boat eighty feet long and seventy feet wide with a big sign on it reading "Caddo Diner." Beer was served on the premises. Since the only way to get to the diner was by water, customers drove to a parking lot, got out of their cars, and took what were called transfer boats or taxi boats over to the diner.

The Caddo Diner prospered and became a popular place to dine, dance, and drink. It was evident that the place needed to be enlarged. Fred says one night the barge was torn loose from its moorings during a storm. "It was replaced with a one-hundred-by-eighty-foot building constructed on pilings."

Others noticed the popularity of the Caddo Diner and went into competition with it. New places sprang up on the Marion County side of Big Cypress Bayou: Crip's, Chartier's, and Keuhn's. All were built on pilings.

"Only the original Caddo Diner could truly have been called a beer boat, but people liked the sound of the term so all the places were called beer boats," says Fred.

Power was supplied to the beer boats by the rural co-op through an overhead power line from the mainland. Jukebox music penetrated the silence of Caddo Lake.

A long-neck bottle of beer was fifteen cents regardless of brand. A soft drink was a nickel. All the catfish you could eat cost seventy-five cents.

"The Caddo Diner opened at eleven o'clock on Thursday morning," says Fred, "and stayed open continuously until midnight Sunday night. Eight waitresses worked there along with four cooks and four taxi boat drivers."

The taxi boats ran day and night year-round. There was no charge for the service, but most people tipped the driver a nickel or dime. The boats were sixteen feet long with flat bottoms equipped with ten-horsepower motors. Each beer boat had its own fleet of taxis, but the owners didn't mind taking passengers to other beer boats.

The beer boats became social centers on Caddo Lake. Parents often brought their children with them and spent a few hours visiting with friends. Some people came in their own boats and tied up at a special mooring area.

Often Fred cruised the lake at night. On two occasions he pulled couples from the water who had just jumped from a taxi boat for the fun of it.

All supplies had to be hauled in by boat. Beer had to be placed directly from the delivery trucks onto the transfer boats. It could not touch the ground in Harrison County. No beer could be brought to the mainland from the beer boats.

The beer boats declined in popularity about the time WWII started. Fred Dahmer writes about the beer boats and other Caddo topics in his book *Caddo Was*.

The crowning glory of Caddo Lake is the yonqupin, rating right alongside cypress trees and Spanish moss as a feature attraction of the lake. It is a plant that produces beautiful blooms in late summer. The large flowers are a creamy yellow color with massive petals. They produce seeds which resemble acorns and are edible if harvested in time. They taste like chestnuts.

Wyatt A. Moore:
Self-styled Riverboat Pilot and Man About Town

Wyatt A. Moore was a major Texas character. He lived at Karnack and knew Caddo Lake perhaps better than anyone else. He traveled in his homemade rowboat (called a Caddo bateau) to such places on the lake as Goat Island, Whistleberry Slough, Whangdoodle Pass, and the Devil's Elbow.

"My bateau is to me what a horse was to a cowboy," said Wyatt. "I couldn't live without it."

His work experience reveals some of his interests. He was a boat operator, commercial fisherman, boatbuilder, farmer, fishing guide, trapper, moonshiner, oil field worker, and water well driller. He was a firearms expert. One of his hobbies was taping funerals on his portable audio cassette recorder. His boat-making ability was featured in an exhibit at the New Orleans World Fair. "I look forward to each day," Wyatt told me once. "I feel that every sun that rises is just for me."

The name of his biography published by UT press is *Every Sun That Rises*. Wyatt was a good customer for the book. He ordered a hundred books to keep at the house for people who wanted to come by and get an autographed copy. "That first hundred books were gone in about three weeks," said Wyatt. "Now I've sold my 800th copy here. The publisher has sent me a few little ol' mineral-right checks along, but I've made more here selling them from my house. Both figures still don't amount to much. I made lots more money moonshining."

Wyatt drank his first whiskey at age eight, when he was gigging fish and hunting for pearls in Caddo Lake. Wyatt lived his life as a grown-up Tom Sawyer. He was always ready for his next adventure on the lake. "It's so big Texas couldn't hold it all," said Wyatt, referring to that part of the lake that is in Louisiana.

Wyatt played a gas hose. It made a shrill noise when he blew through it. "It's just a regular gas hose like you would find in any hardware store, the type you connect from a stove

to a gas jet." He won a trophy in the fire-ant-calling contest at Marshall by blowing his gas hose.

He thought his walk through the twentieth century was a happy stroll. He always considered himself an independent operator, regardless of the type of work he was doing.

When he was moonshining, he made good use of his Caddo bateau. "Revenuers didn't hunt moonshiners on the water," said Wyatt. He established his operation on the south end of the lake and sold his whiskey during the twenties and thirties until liquor was legalized. He operated alone and didn't have any partners. That's probably one reason he wasn't caught. He kept a 110-gallon still and six mash barrels going constantly. He sold about 150 gallons a month at three dollars a gallon. He says it cost about fifty cents a gallon to make.

"I guess I was the best loop-holer the game wardens ever met up with," bragged Wyatt. "Lawyers call them technicalities. Us common criminals call 'em loopholes. The game wardens would nearly catch me, but I knew there was a loophole somewhere and I'd squirm through it."

He was an amazing handyman. "I used to hardly buy anything. I'd go to the hardware store and ask about an item. The clerk would tell me he didn't have it but would be glad to order it. I told him I didn't want to buy it, I just wanted to see it so I could make one like it."

Wyatt had a good friend named Shine Hale. When Shine died a couple of years ago, Wyatt wrote his epitaph: "When he is dead and in his grave, no more liquor will he crave. Upon his tomb will be wrote, 'a million gallons went down his throat.'"

East Texas Moonshine

San Augustine County used to have a place called "No Man's Land." Clarence Fountain knows about it.

"They made whiskey there. That's all they done. Made

whiskey. Made it for a living. First time I made it I made it on a syrup bucket with an air gun pipe. Half pint at a time. And I sold it from here to Lubbock, Texas, one hundred or two hundred gallons at a time. Ten dollars a gallon. I made more money than all the farmers together here. I farmed, too. But I made whiskey at night. Had to. And I had two of the best bull-dogs that ever walked. I'd put one on this side of the branch, one on the other side, and nobody came down there. I didn't need no gun.

"I got caught five times. They got my still five times. But I never paid a nickel out for a fine in my life. I was tried only once and I came clear. They got to where they'd just come out here and pick me up. Take me to jail. That's how come me to quit. But I didn't quit. I'm knowed everywhere, I guess. I can't walk in three beer joints in Houston without somebody knowin' me."

The basic ingredient in Clarence's moonshine was corn. He would take an ear of corn and slice it into pieces called chops.

"It takes fifty pounds of chops and fifty pounds of sugar to the barrel. You get five gallons of whiskey to a barrel. Good whiskey. Why, there used to be a ten-gallon keg of whiskey settin' in every man's living room or kitchen. We used copper cookers then. I mean good 'uns."

Jethro Holmes also worked in "No Man's Land."

"I'm eighty-four years old and I was born and raised in San Augustine County, and we raised cattle and hogs, horses and mules. We had our own farm and raised tobacco and cotton, corn, peas, and goobers."

Jethro was one of the most reliable moonshiners in all of East Texas.

"It came by birth, I'll say. My great-grandfather came from North Carolina in the early days of settlin' Texas, and he was forty-two years old and he'd never been married, and he brought twelve settlers to Texas in ox wagons. He died at one hundred and four years old. Claimed whiskey killed him."

Jethro says the best whiskey is made from rye.

"You take the very best rye, forty pounds of rye to a fifty-gallon barrel, and cover the rye with four inches of water. Let it stay there all night. Next morning fill the barrel almost full of warm water and put in fifty pounds of sugar. In about four days, it's ready to be run off. Your still should be made out of stainless steel or copper. We had two barrels goin' all time, practically. Cooked 'em over a hickory fire. We generally made about eighteen gallons a week. They paid me fifty dollars for a five-gallon keg. I drank almost a quart a day for sixteen years. I had six men working for me and I delivered whiskey

to Tyler, Longview, Kilgore, Gladewater, Dallas, and Fort Worth."

The whiskey came out about 200 proof, real strong. They'd cut it down with water.

Wild hogs were always around a still site and ate the corn residue when it was poured out of the still. One time a hog, hungry for corn, climbed into the barrel and drowned. But they went ahead and cooked it off. Customers complained of the whiskey being a little greasy.

Moonshine in the Shade

Bill O'Neal teaches history at Panola College in Carthage. Once he asked his students if they could find any old bootleggers or moonshiners who would allow themselves to be interviewed.

"I knew this had been a center of the moonshine industry when it was in its heyday," says Bill. "The students found forty-four people who had either made or sold illegal hooch. Seven of them insisted on remaining anonymous, and several others would give us only their nicknames: Black Jack, Mr. Monk, Mr. Sam, and so forth."

Bill has a map showing the 254 counties in Texas and the

number of stills seized in each one between 1939 and 1973. Many West Texas counties have none whatever. There's a lot of smoke connected with a still, and the smoke is pretty hard to hide in West Texas, because the land is flat and you can see great distances. The East Texas pine forests, however, are a perfect place to make white lightning, because the smoke can be concealed. Most of the counties in East Texas had twenty or so stills. But Marion County had more than 200. Harrison County holds the record, with 788 stills seized.

Once a couple of young men were arrested for a minor offense and placed in jail in Longview. They worked as trusties to pay off their fine. One day they discovered large quantities of a clear liquid stored in bottles in a small room. When they inquired about it, they were told it was moonshine. The two trusties started selling the stuff. They would take liquor from a bottle and replace it with water. The bottles always looked full. The pair got away with it and raised enough money to pay their fines and get out of jail.

Now, the deputies had been using that stuff as antifreeze. So when they started pouring what they thought to be highly charged alcohol but was actually water into their radiators, several sheriff's cars ended up with cracked blocks.

One lady was making gin in her bathtub. She saw the sheriff coming up the road, so she poured bubble bath into her tub and hopped in. When the sheriff busted in the door, she invited him to search the house for any illegal drinking substance. He didn't find a thing.

Another woman perfected the technique of hiding a flat bottle between her legs. She would sneak the stuff in and out of establishments and no one was the wiser.

Once a man and his wife were delivering some shine over to Marshall and a sheriff's car started after them. A rip-roaring chase ensued. The wife was driving while the husband drank the evidence. By the time the sheriff caught up with them, it had all disappeared.

Near Gary, not far from Carthage, a man had a still in the woods, and the sheriff and some deputies rushed the house. He had only one bottle of booze on the place. So as he ran by the wood-burning cookstove, he threw it in. The stove exploded and blew the clothes off his wife. His four kids came running out of the house and hopped in a barrel, and the barrel tipped over and rolled down a hill. Everybody came out okay. The sheriff left shaking his head.

The homemade brew sold for two to three dollars a gallon. One independent operator traded one hundred gallons of his stuff for a car. That was about a month's output.

East Texans depend on Mother Nature to give them signs to predict the weather. Some watch the habits of birds and animals:

- The chattering of flying squirrels in midwinter indicates an early spring.
- Severe weather can be expected when migrating birds wing south early.
- If the cat basks in February sun, it will warm itself by the stove in March.
- The early arrival of cranes in the fall indicates a cold winter.
- When squirrels are seldom seen in the fall, a cold winter is anticipated.
- When summer birds fly away, summer goes, too.
- If crows wing south, a cold winter will follow; if they fly north, the opposite is true.

Planting by the Signs

Let there be light in the firmament of the heavens to divide the day from night, and let them be for signs and for seasons, and for days and years. Genesis 1:14.

To everything there is a season, and a time for every purpose under the heavens: a time to be born and a time to die, a time to plant and a time to pluck up that which is planted. Ecclesiastes 3:1-2.

Planting and harvesting have to be done according to the

signs—so say some East Texans. Other activities that work better when done by the signs are timber cutting, slaughtering, weaving, painting, and castrating cattle. There is a part of the human body associated with each sign. Many farmers credit their success by following the signs, which come around every twenty-eight days.

Some almanacs say peanuts planted at the right time will grow faster and produce a fuller crop. If planted on the wrong sign, growth will be slower and vines will be thinner. Wheat and other things that grow seed heads will be a third larger than if planted at the wrong time. Potato crops will be three to five times bigger if planted at the right time.

Okra, planted at the right time, will start bearing when it gets four or five inches high. If planted at the wrong time, it might not bear at all.

Almanacs are full of advice on all facets of life: advertise when the signs are in Libra or Scorpio. Ask for jobs or deal with creditors when the signs are in Leo, Libra, or Scorpio. Cut hair to stimulate growth of it when the signs are in Cancer, Scorpio, or Pisces. Country folks fish and pull their teeth according to the signs.

People read their almanacs each month to know what to do during the whole year. Before radio, farmers really depended on the almanac to forecast the weather.

One woman always cuts her rosebushes back on February 14, and she always has beautiful roses. Another woman says February is a good time to plant beets, peas, lettuce, onions, radishes, spinach, and turnips. Plant the things that make on top of the ground on the first quarter of the moon when the signs are in the arms (Twins). Plant things that make under the ground on the decreasing of the moon and the signs are in the knees (Goat). This is also a good time to kill weeds or prepare soil for planting. Never plant anything on the new moon, and do not plant on the day that the moon changes.

The *Ladies Birthday Almanac* regulated many

lives in the early days. Mr. T. E. Black of Alabama wrote a book on living by the signs, and it is in several East Texas homes.

D. D. Chadwick offers this planting guide:

Plant corn on the full moon; cotton, beans, and peas on twin days; don't plant on virgin days; plant spuds on dark nights; plant anything on the Bowman (Archer) sign.

"You plant watermelon when the sign is in the highs and you'll have long, smooth watermelons. You plant them in Scorpion days and they'll be rotten, have a rotten spot in them."

Fishing Signs

When is the best time to fish? Bacon said "Every wind has its weather." Sir Izaak Walton said it even better:

> When the wind is in the north,
> The skillful fisher goes not forth;
> When the wind is in the east,
> 'Tis good for neither man nor beast;
> When the wind is in the south,
> It blows the flies in the fish's mouth;
> When the wind is in the west,
> There it is the very best.

Here's another version:

when the barometer is high or rising
when a storm is imminent
after a brief storm at any time of the
    year
during a steady, light rain
when rain has just stopped
when the wind is from the south or
    west
when the moon is between the new
    and the full
when water is clear
when water is murky
on an overcast day
when water is rising
when a lake starts to drop
when oak leaves are the size of
    squirrel ears
when the dogwood blossoms
when ants build high mounds
when spiderwebs are taut
when cattle are up and grazing
    (Old-timers say if they're resting,
    that's what the fish are doing)

at the crack of dawn during hot, dry months
on a calm evening for bass and trout
on stormy days during warm months
after the first thunderstorm of spring.

Fishing with a Telephone

Charley Eckhardt knows about a type of fishing called telephoning. "Take the guts out of an old crank telephone and hook a wire to each contact and drop them over the side of the boat and then give that telephone a crank," says Charley. "The electric current will stun the fish and they'll come to the top of the water. Don't try it in an aluminum boat."

Charley also knows about "shining" fish. "What they used to do was get a gallon jug of busthead whiskey and go to the head of the creek and dump that busthead in. The fish would all get drunk and swim around on their bellies and you could dip them up.

"It works beautifully. 'Course, moonshine whiskey is mighty expensive these days to do that."

Charley knows about a guy named Dobbin who used to dynamite fish: "Dobbin was the greatest fisherman in all of East Texas. He was known as the finest and most successful dynamiter east of the Brazos. Everybody knew it.

"They'd hear this big BOOM back in the woods and they'd all know Dobbin was out fishing.

"The sheriff would hear the BOOM, too. Later he'd go by Dobbin's house to find Dobbin cleaning fish. There'd be a trotline hanging there, wet. When the sheriff would ask about how Dobbin caught the fish, Dobbin would reply, 'Trotline.'

"Now, they couldn't get a conviction on old Dobbin. But they hired some new lawmen to do nothing but enforce game laws. They called 'em game wardens.

"They didn't hire any college boys in those days. They got some of the best fish dynamiters and fish poachers in all of Texas to catch the rest of them.

"They hired one game warden just to catch old Dobbin. One morning Dobbin came out of his house, looked around, couldn't see any sign of this feller, and decided to go fishing.

"So he went and got him a bushel basket and a stick of dynamite, and started into the woods. The game warden was hiding behind a bush and started following Dobbin.

"Dobbin got to a water hole in the middle of the woods that he knew had fish in it. He puts down his bushel basket, takes out his dynamite, and about that time the game warden jumps out and starts to arrest Dobbin.

"Dobbin told the game warden he was going to blow up a stump and put the chips in the basket to use as kindling during the winter.

"The game warden reached over and grabbed Dobbin's stick of dynamite. Dobbin was smoking a corncob pipe all this time. He just kind of slipped it out of his mouth and touched the fire from his pipe to the fuse on the dynamite.

"The game warden was ranting and raving and didn't notice that the stick of dynamite he had in his hand was about to explode.

"Dobbin told the game warden he oughta be careful with that dynamite, that somebody was gonna be hurt.

"There wasn't anyplace to throw the dynamite but in the waterhole. And that's where he threw it.

"After the echoes from the BOOM died down, and the water quit raining down, Dobbin looked at him and asked what they should do with all the fish he had killed."

Dowsing

Water dowsing is widely practiced in East Texas. The gift of dowsing is the ability of a person to locate underground sources of water or minerals while carrying in his hands a Y-shaped stick called a dowsing rod or divining rod. Other terms synonymous with dowsing are *doodlebugging, striking, water witching, radiesthesia,* and *rhabdomancy.*

Over the ages the most popular rods have been made from peach trees, although maple, persimmon, willow, poison oak, and plum trees have also served. Divining rods have been made from materials other than wood, such as ox horn, ivory, gold, silver, and whalebone. Dowsers seem to have had equal

success with bent coat hangers, watch springs, scissors, or pliers.

The dowsing rod, usually about a foot long, is generally a forked branch, one side of which is held in each hand. The middle or long stem is pointed upward. Some dowsers carry the rod with their palms up, some with their palms down. When the rod is carried over a spot where underground water is hidden, the pointed end is attracted downward. Some dowsers can tell you how deep the water is, the direction of the flow, and how strong it is. This information comes from the number of times the long end of the rod bobs up and down.

Some families say it is a special gift handed down from one generation to another, while others believe it is a learned art. Some people can find water with a rod, others can't.

Some dowsers are drained after finding a stream of water and feel physically exhausted. That's why dowsers find only three to four wells a day.

Some water witches find water, other find gold, silver, or bone. They put a little of what they're looking for on the end of their diving rod and it seeks out more of the same substance.

The birthplace of modern-day dowsing was in the Harz mountains of Germany, where the most advanced mining practices were developed. Miners believed that metallic ores attracted certain trees, causing them to lean over the spot where the ore lay underground. A branch of such a tree would be cut so that it might be observed where else it drooped. Later, a branch was cut for each hand, their extremities being tied together. Finally, as a matter of convenience, a forked branch was cut and an end grasped in each hand with the palms upward. A common practice in those times was to bury money for safekeeping. So the rod functioned as a detector of buried treasure as well as of metallic lodes.

Churches held that the power of dowsing meant an affiliation with the Devil. Those persons found engaged in mysterious practices risked being burned at the stake for sorcery. In Germany, dowsing was enveloped with religious ceremonies and prayers as a shield against persecution. In an effort to prove that both operator and rod were not under demoniac influence but were recipients of a divine gift, elaborate rituals were observed.

The dowser would purify himself through fasts, novenas, and sexual abstention. Rods would be cut only on holy days. The rod, wrapped in swaddling clothes, was to be carried to the church for baptism and laid in the bed of a newly baptized infant, by whose name it was thereafter to be addressed.

The type of wood meant something, too. Hazel was best in searching for silver, ash twigs for copper, pitch pine for lead and tin, and tips of iron and steel for finding gold.

Indians didn't know about dowsing until it was introduced into North America by European settlers. By the late 1700s, dowsing had become associated in America with witchcraft, which is why the practice became known in America as water witching.

The Possum

The only native marsupial is the opossum. It was the first pouch-bearer that western civilization encountered. From 1500 onward it was a subject of amazement and growing surmise, inspiring poetry, fables, folklore, and legends.

Captain John Smith of the Jamestown colony in Virginia was responsible for the name by which it is known. *Opossum* is a rendering of the Algonquian Indian word *apasum*, meaning "white animal," for the opossum has a pointed face covered with soft white hair. In most parts of the country it's commonly known as the "possum."

While the possum has poor eyesight, its long snout provides the animal with a strong sense of smell. The snout is of major importance when foraging for food.

The possum waddles along in a shuffling gait on short legs but is adept at climbing. The five toes of the front feet have sharp white claws. The big toe on the hind feet, nail-less and flexible, serves as a thumb, enabling the possum to grasp branches firmly.

The tail, covered with scales, is of great value when the animal is traversing a tree limb. Should the branch be shaken and the possum slip, the tail immediately tightens, safely anchoring the animal. Young possums, weighing little, suspend themselves more easily than do adults. The possum uses its tail to carry wads of Spanish moss for making nests.

People find the tail a convenience when picking up the animal, using it as a handle. When being transported by it, the opossum is capable of climbing up its own tail and will bite the hand holding it. One should carry the animal by the tail with one hand and firmly seize the nape of the neck with the other.

The possum lives along creek beds where hunting and fishing are good. Pregnancy for the possum is a scant twelve days and eighteen hours. The babies are extremely premature at birth and seek the haven of their mother's pouch, which acts as a kind of incubator while they are continuing to develop.

The babies are so tiny at birth that the entire litter of eighteen or twenty could nest in a teaspoon. The internal organs are visible through the skin, and eyes and ears are not yet completely formed.

Once safely inside the pouch, the little ones explore for a nipple. The luckier ones quickly attach themselves to it with the aid of their powerful tongues. Sucking starts immediately, and within an hour the nipple's length is doubled.

Little by little the nipple becomes elongated, acting not only as a conduit for nourishment but also as a tether for wider mobility. For weeks the baby possums cling constantly to the teats.

During hunting trips the mother closes her pouch to prevent the babies from toppling out. She searches the treetops for birds and their eggs. Possums are good swimmers and keep the young ones warm and dry inside the pouch.

Before long the babies are mature enough to leave the pouch and view the world from their mother's back, clinging to her coarse fur. During the days following weaning, they are most vulnerable as prey for hawks, owls, coyotes, bobcats, foxes, and wolves. At three months the little possums are capable of fending for themselves.

Possums eat insects, moles, mice, snakes, lizards, frogs, crayfish, snails, fish, birds and their eggs, mushrooms, berries, grapes, apples, persimmons, pawpaws, greenbrier, field corn, and even carrion.

When cornered, the possum bares its many teeth, which are set in powerful jaws. While confronting an antagonist, it coils and uncoils its tail. Its customary means of protection is feigning death, or "playing possum." Some people believe the possum is paralyzed with fright. When the enemy leaves the scene, the possum returns to its normal state.

The possum's white flesh has long been considered palatable but fat by country people. Possums are easily caught in traps but are not nearly as savory as the ones hauled down from a tree. The trauma of injury produces changes in the body which influence the flavor of the meat. There are several possum recipes, but nearly all of them say that sweet potatoes are essential to a possum feast.

The animal is not recommended as a pet because of its small brain, dirty personal habits, and repellent odor.

The 'Coon

The raccoon, better known in most places as "coon," exists nowhere in the world but in North America. Since much of the raccoon's diet comes from the water, it generally makes its nest in forest areas less than a mile from a stream or lake. It prefers to reside high in a hollow tree.

Though a nocturnal meanderer and hunter, by day it enjoys draping itself in the crotch of a tree to sunbathe. Surefooted in trees, it uses them not only as lodging but as a haven when threatened.

Although an excellent tree-climber, the raccoon is not a swift runner. When hunted, it relies on clever tactics invented spontaneously to fit the circumstances. Intelligence compensates for its lack of speed. An old, wise 'coon has been known to draw a pursuing dog into water, climb on its head, and drown it.

Often as cunning as a fox, the raccoon may destroy its trail by wading along the edge of a stream or crossing fallen logs. It will even dive into water as a last recourse. When cornered, it defends itself by cutting and slashing at its attacker.

A relative of the giant panda, the raccoon's pointed face is marked with a black band across the cheeks and eyes and a streak running from forehead to nose. The black mask serves as protective coloration, making the black eyes more difficult to detect in a fight. The fur coloring ranges from gray to brown and blackish. Six or seven black bands ring the yellow-gray tail.

The raccoon has a dainty way of eating, facilitated by delicate front paws equipped with long, marvelously dexterous fingers. Its diet varies from freshwater foods to nuts and fruits, vegetables, and birds and their eggs. It customarily washes muddy frogs, turtles, crayfish, and clams prior to consuming them.

Science has given the 'coon the Latin name *lotor,* meaning "the washer." Its name in German is *Waschbar.*

In April the raccoon's undercoat becomes less heavy and the outer guard hairs thinner. The first signs of the developing winter coat become evident in late August.

In East Texas 'coons mate during December. Nine weeks later, four to five blind young are born, complete with masks and furry coats. At three weeks their eyes are open, and at two months they are able to sally forth on short hunting trips with their mother.

At sunset mother and her young go to the edge of a stream to explore shallow pools for their favorite food, crayfish. Their tapering, agile fingers slip over rocks to reveal insects, mussels, and snails. 'Coon babies are instructed in the delicate art of catching frogs and slower-swimming fish. Slippery earthworms that emerge after a summer shower are easily picked up with their long black fingers.

Crumbling rotten logs are investigated for grubs, crickets are pounced upon in the grass, fragile-shelled turtle eggs are dug from nests, and the eggs of ground-nesting birds are discovered. Periodically a raccoon family will raid cornfields. 'Coons also enjoy berries, grapes, and pecans. In other words, they enjoy their favorite foods but when they're not available will eat something else.

The mother keeps the cubs by her side for nearly a year. They travel long distances while foraging for food. When danger strikes, the mother will lead her young up a tree and then dash away, luring the dogs after her. The polygamous father assumes no responsibility for his offspring and lives alone.

When sensing trouble, the raccoon makes a noise somewhere between a hiss and a snort. It can also purr like a cat, though its usual talk is a churring, birdlike sound. Some dark night when your ears are assailed by the eerie call of a screech owl coming not from a tree but from the ground, its source may not be an owl.

Trappers have found that 'coons are attracted by bright, shiny objects. They take advantage of this trait by attaching tinfoil to their traps.

Country people value raccoon oil as an aid to keeping leather in prime condition. It has also served as a lubricant for machinery. The skins have been used as barter, and raccoon meat is very palatable.

Life Span of Animals in Years

bat	3-5	goat	15-20
mouse	3-5	deer	18-25
snail	8	pig	20
fox	8-10	bear	20-30
rabbit	8-10	horse	20-35
squirrel	8-10	lizard	25
wolf	10-15	large snake	25
beaver	12	toad	30
dog	15	crocodile	40-50 plus
cat	15-20		

Life Span of Birds in Years:

wren	3	nightingale	18
thrush	10	crane	24
blackbird	10	crow	25-30
robin	10	skylark	30
pheasant	15	hawk	40
partridge	15	pelican	50
goldfinch	15	goose	70
blackcap	15	heron	80
lark	18		

Plants

Plants have been used as food, drink, flavoring, cosmetics, perfume, and dyes. People years ago believed that effective medicines must have an offensive smell and bitter taste. Often medicinal plants were chosen at first because of their rank odor and were found later actually to contain beneficial properties.

For the relief of headaches, aromatic flowers were held to temples and forehead. Some were applied to wounds to hasten healing. Bay leaves in bath water had a soothing effect on sore and aching bodies. Powdered leaves of alehoof, chamomile, peppermint, and thyme were used as snuff to cure head colds and relieve depression.

As protection against disease, people fumigated their homes with fragrant substances such as sage, rosemary, cinnamon, and thyme. Rue was particularly popular because it repelled fleas. Sufferers of insomnia slept on pillows stuffed with hops. Beside exuding a pleasant scent, the hops exerted a gentle narcotic influence that induced sleep.

Strongly aromatic leaves and resins are said to possess antibiotic properties. So potent is the antiseptic quality of the oil from thyme leaves that in the past it was applied to soldiers' uniforms to protect them from vermin.

Doctors customarily carried aromatics at the upper tips of their walking sticks, which they frequently raised to their noses as discreetly as possible when tending the sick.

Such plants as thyme, sage, chamomile, basil, lavender, and hyssop were scattered on the floors of churches and other places where people, usually unbathed, congregated in large numbers.

In courts of law, judges were presented with aromatic flowers to counteract the offensive odors of unwashed prisoners.

Potpourris were an old-fashioned way of scenting musty houses. Mixtures of rose petals, lavender, rosemary, thyme, cloves, and dried orange peel were placed in potpourri jars made of china or wood. Holes in the jars' lids released the aroma. A properly made batch of potpourri could last fifty years.

The most fragrant flowers are white. In general, with the increase of pigment in the petals the aroma of perfume lessens. The best time to gather flower petals is at dawn, before the sun evaporates the oils.

Early settlers were concerned with basic survival. Perfume was considered frivolous. Females wearing perfumes for the purpose of attracting men were dunked.

Benefits of the Sassafras Tree

"Ever since I can remember, we've had sassafras tea."

Bertie Childs of Center drinks sassafras tea, which is made from roots of the sassafras tree.

"Well, we keep it all year. We dig it in the spring, let it dry a little bit, then freeze it. Whenever I want it, I go get it."

She cuts the root into small pieces, two or three inches long, designed to fit in a pot or pan.

"And I usually use about three or four pieces of root. Then I pour in the water, put it on the stove, and let it start boiling."

She saves the roots to use when she makes another batch of tea.

"You can use the same roots several times. Just add more water."

Sassafras trees grow throughout East Texas. They are aromatic members of the laurel family and yield a soft yellow wood and yellow flowers. The dried bark on the root is used for flavoring. It will also make you sweat a lot. The tree produces an oil used in perfumes.

"So many people will plant these trees just for the foliage in the fall. They are beautiful trees. They don't grow to be so tall like an oak or pine, but they have spectacular autumn leaves."

Sassafras tea has several uses.

"Everybody has different reasons for using it. Some people take it for the medicinal benefits. We drink it because we like it."

Root beer is made from the root of the sassafras tree. Sassafras tea has sort of a root beer flavor. Bertie likes to drink her tea hot, while most people prefer it cold.

Sassafras tea is a common spring tonic in East Texas.

"They say it thins your blood. Some families wouldn't think of starting the spring season without a few glasses of sassafras tea."

The tree has three different types of leaves. One is shaped like a left-handed mitten, another like a right-handed mitten. The third is a combination of the other two. Some leaves are used to make filé (fee-lay) in gumbo. It's a thickener.

"Indians started that. They used the leaves to thicken their soup. You dry them, then crush them. They have a flavor like the roots, but not enough to bother the food."

Hints from Homemakers

There are several homemade products for getting rid of cockroaches:

1. Mash two-thirds of a pound of plaster of Paris, add a little sugar, and mix with one pound of oatmeal. Place in areas most frequented by cockroaches.
2. Fill jars partly full of stale beer. Prop sticks against their sides. The roaches, attracted to the beer, will mount the sticks and fall into the jars.
3. Combine one ounce of red lead with a half-pint of corn-meal moistened with molasses to a batterlike consistency. Spread it on thin pieces of board. Cockroaches will digest the fatal mixture.
4. Mix equal amounts of borax and brown sugar in a dish and place it where the cockroaches are most frequently seen.

To destroy crickets, put Scotch snuff into their holes. Not everybody wants to destroy crickets, because their music is a symbol of peace and contentment in the country.

There are more than 22,000 species of crickets in the world today, the most common of which is the black field cricket. This little musician, when heard in English homes, was said to bring good luck. In both China and Japan, valued for its music, it was often kept as a pet in cages. During the years of the Chinese empire, crickets were carefully tended in the royal palace. Their cages were works of art, and many are preserved in today's museums.

Cricket is a word formed in imitation of the creature's call. The insect should be termed an instrumentalist, not a

singer, for it produces sound by rubbing parts of its body together, not by forcing air between vocal chords. The wings of the two sexes differ in that the male's alone are characterized by the file and scraper for sound-making.

A heavy vein at the front of each forewing has a rasplike surface of numerous ridges on the underside; a smooth rib on the upper side of the wing serves as a scraper. The cricket raises its forewings to a forty-five-degree angle and moves one across the other, like a bow and fiddle, to make music.

The taut wing membranes act as a sounding board so that the chirping can be heard at surprising distances.

There is a direct relationship between temperature and call rates. During cool weather it is slower; when the mercury rises, the tempo increases. Though most of the cricket's sounds are to attract a mate or establish its territory, some are thought to be for the sheer joy of living.

The cricket seldom flies, but projects itself through the air in great leaps by the aid of its powerfully muscled hind legs. They are equipped with spikes that dig into the ground for traction, enabling it to jump remarkable distances for its size. The little creature is as capable of propelling itself through water as it is of leaping about on land.

The cricket menu is varied: vegetables, seeds, grain, meat, rubber, and clothing—the sweatier the better.

The insect listens with its legs, since its auditory organs are small, elongated apertures on the front legs.

The life span of the cricket is short, stretching from early summer to the first heavy frost.

Scarecrows

A stuffed shirt and pants propped upright is used to scare crows away from crops. Another way is to string kernels of corn on long horsehairs and scatter them over the cornfields. Upon swallowing them, the crow will make such a raucous noise as he tries to free his throat of the corn that the other birds will be driven away, sometimes for the season. Some early East Texas farmers made imitation hawks to scare away birds. They stuck turkey feathers in a potato and hung it from a tall, bent pole. Wind agitated it, making it even more realistic.

Country Cures

Horehound, nightshade, May apple root, snakeroot, sassafras bark, black haw roots, poke root, peach tree leaves, inner bark of the oak, slippery elm bark, inner bark of pine trees, resin, and wild cherry tree bark were all used for home remedies. The base for the mixture was either tallow for making salve or honey for making cough syrups and other medicines. They used vinegar from apples.

For a break in the arm or leg, settlers used clay made up in a dough with vinegar. They would daub that on the limb and let it set for twenty-eight days, then break it off, and the arm or leg would be back in place.

Alcoholism: Have the patient eat an owl's egg. Place a live minnow in his bottle of spirits and let it die there.

Arthritis: Massage the areas with a mixture of whiskey, chloroform, and wintergreen four times a day. Eat one-half pound of fresh cherries daily.

Bad breath: Rub the gums with wool coated with honey.

Bruises: Apply a paste of butter and chopped parsley to bruises.

Burns: Make a poultice of oatmeal and cold water.

Childbirth: When labor is prolonged, blow snuff, held on a goose feather, up the mother's nose. This will induce a sneezing fit, resulting in delivery.

Colic: Drink a mixture of brewed catnip leaves and milk.

Corns: Bind on bread soaked in vinegar.

Deafness: Drop a mixture of onion juice and ant eggs into the ear.

Diarrhea: Drink brewed peach tree leaves.

Hair: To make hair thicker, massage the juice of watercress into the scalp. Lighten hair by making a rinse of chopped rhubarb roots. Darken with a mixture of black walnut hulls, powdered cloves, and alcohol.

Hay fever: Crush fresh milkweed in cheesecloth and inhale.

Headache: Apply a poultice of grated uncooked potato to the forehead.

Irritable infant: Onion tea.

Itching: Bathe with soap and water, scrubbing with a corncob.

Nettle sting: Rub with mint, sage leaves, or rosemary.

Nosebleed: Chew paper.

Poison Ivy: Rub brewed poke roots on the sores.

Ringworm: Apply a mixture of gunpowder and vinegar.

Snake bite: Kill a chicken, cut it open, and place it on the wound.

Sore throat: Gargle with a mixture of salt, powdered alum, vinegar, and the water from one boiled red pepper.

Splinters: Apply raw bacon.

Tapeworm: Drink tea made from pumpkinseeds.

Toothache: Chew catnip.

Warts: Rub them with green walnuts or bacon rind.

Wounds: Apply fresh, warm cow dung.

Pioneer Resourcefulness

Early East Texans took up residence in a place that depended on human ingenuity to get along. The trees, streams, berries, and wild game provided dietary sustenance as well as material for making things. East Texans also learned how to be frugal and careful about what they threw away. They thought something once discarded had several other uses.

An old pair of bib overalls made an excellent backpack. Just tie a knot in each leg and the pack is ready to be loaded. The suspenders were slipped over the wearer's shoulders.

The fireplace was a source of heat that was used for warmth and cooking. A thick bed of ashes was kept in the fireplace to help conserve wood. The red-hot coals were covered with ashes to last through the night, even well into the following day. Uncover the ashes and the fire can be easily re-kindled with just a couple of swishes with a poking rod.

The pioneers made candy out of the white leaves found on a horehound plant. They made paper from fibrous plants that grow in the woods and meadows. They dyed fabrics with berries, onion skins, and insects. The women made quilts from scraps of material. They braided their own rugs. The men made bricks from clay. They tanned their own animal skins and made chair bottoms and ropes from rawhide. They made candles from paraffin and beeswax.

Those early settlers were savvy, too. They knew that if they chipped holes in ice they should first warm the blade near a fire or blow on it. A cold blade, being very brittle, could easily break.

They tied their own fishing flies and made colorful lures. They made bean bags, kites, and tops for children. They made shampoos by mixing olive oil, an egg, some lemon juice, and apple cider vinegar. Pulverized almonds, cucumbers, watercress, and lettuce were used to make skin lotions. Sunburn was treated with an egg white and a teaspoon of castor oil. Baking soda and salt were used as a toothpaste. For flavor, add drops of peppermint or wintergreen oil.

For an old-fashioned beauty bath, boil four quarts of rain-water with one pound each of barley, bran, oatmeal, bay leaves, dried flowers, and brown rice mixed in.

To make lye, pioneers dripped water through ashes. They mixed the lye with grease and water to create soap. To get rid of mice, they mixed cornmeal and cement and placed it in containers where mice would run.

They made pipes from corncobs and grew tobacco to smoke in them. Gourds were used to make all kinds of containers. Feathers from crow, eagle, hawk, owl, and turkeys were used to make writing instruments. They simply sharpened the tips of feathers to a point and dipped them in ink.

The Dairy

Butter-making begins with the care of cows. Some farmers believe that a steady diet of corn fodder does not produce good butter, so they use a blend of half bran and half cornmeal. Others say a twice-daily feeding of early-cut hay and a mixture of scalded cornmeal and wheat bran, moistened with sweet skimmed milk, is the best diet a cow could have.

To make cream, fresh milk was strained through a cloth and poured into deep tin pails either standing in vessels of ice or maintained at low temperatures by cold springwater running through the milkhouse—if the building was so favorably situated. Cream-setting lasted for a period of twenty-four hours or more. The ideal temperature for cream at churning time was 57 degrees. After being skimmed from the pails, the cream was put in a churn and worked for twelve to twenty minutes.

The cylindrical dash churn, with a stick handle protruding through the top, was generally made of pottery and powered by hand. To each twenty pounds of butter, three ounces of white sugar and six ounces of salt were added.

In the absence of pasturage during winter months, butter generally lacked sufficient yellow, so it was dyed with seeds, turmeric, or carrot juice.

When the butter was formed, the buttermilk reserves were drained off for cooking purposes. The butter was then transferred to a bowl.

Corn

Hominy is an Indian word meaning "parched corn." To make hominy, first shuck some ears of firm, dried corn. Take off the underdeveloped kernels from either end of the cob and shell the corn by hand.

Put the kernels into an iron vessel and cover them with cold water. Add one and a half tablespoons of lye to every gallon of corn. Boil until the husks start to separate from the kernels.

Transfer the corn to another vessel and wash it seven or eight times in clear, cold water. Rinse out the first pot to prevent sticking when the hominy is boiled again later.

To completely remove the husks, put the kernels in a course-mashed sieve. Wear rubber gloves to protect hands from the lye. Run a forceful stream of water on the corn, at the same time rubbing it over the mash.

After husking, return the corn to the iron vessel and boil in fresh water until tender. Hominy can be canned for future consumption and is usually eaten after frying it in bacon drippings. It can also be eaten just salted like boiled peanuts.

In the old days, hominy was chiefly made during the winter months when country folks had fewer farm chores.

Dough Starters

Some dough starters, kept active for more than a hundred years, have been handed down from one generation to the next like precious family heirlooms. For one called "Buttermilk Yeast," ingredients include one quart of buttermilk flour, one-half cup of sugar, one cup yeast, and three pints of water.

The recipe calls for the buttermilk to be heated at midday. When it starts to boil, put in the yeast and sugar. Stir, adding enough flour to form a stiff batter. Allow to stand in a warm spot until nightfall. Then add two and a half cups of water and allow it to stand until the following morning. Add the rest of the water, and the buttermilk yeast is ready for bread-making.

Cornbread and Coffee

Cornbread is one staple that every East Texas house had in ready supply. People ate it at every meal. For snacks, and sometimes as a complete meal, they ate cornbread crumpled up in a glass of milk.

The recipe for country cornbread is to blend thoroughly a cup of flour, a cup of cornmeal, four teaspoons of baking powder, two eggs, one and a half cups of sweet milk, a tablespoon of cooking oil, and a teaspoon of salt. Bake in a greased pan at four hundred degrees for thirty minutes or until crusty and brown. There are recipe variations that include buttermilk, honey, and molasses among the ingredients.

Those hearty souls that tamed East Texas spread apple butter on their breads. They also made butters from cherries, honey, lemons, peaches, peanuts, plums, pumpkins, rhubarb, and tomatoes.

They made coffee from sunflower seeds. They first crushed them with a rolling pin, then dropped them into a vessel containing water. The kernels sank; the hulls floated.

The seeds were used for snack food. They cooked the empty sunflower seed hulls in a skillet until brown, then put them through a grain mill. They used one teaspoon (or an amount suitable to individual taste) of ground hulls to each cup of water. It was then steeped for three minutes. If they so desired, they sweetened it with honey.

Coffee was also made from chicory, barley, chick-peas, dandelion root, bran, and almonds. Teas were made from mint or wild strawberry sprigs.

Delicacies from Weeds and Pigs' Feet

Some East Texas homes served dandelion wine. Folks gathered a gallon of dandelion heads in the morning while they were still fresh with dew. They put them in a two-gallon crock, poured in boiling water, spread a piece of cheesecloth over the mouth of the crock, and left it for three days at room temperature.

They squeezed the juice from the flower blossoms and threw them away, saving the liquid. They poured this into a large vessel and added three pounds of sugar, three chopped lemons, and four chopped oranges. They covered the pot and boiled the ingredients for half an hour. Then they let it cool down to lukewarm, poured it into a crock, and added two tablespoons of yeast. It was covered with cheesecloth and allowed to stand for two or three weeks. When the bubbling stopped, it was ready to filter through cheesecloth and bottle.

Canning took place during late summer when

vegetables and fruits were at their peak. The asparagus, beans, beets, carrots, corn, greens, mushrooms, okra, peas, and potatoes were cooked for a few minutes and placed in jars which were filled with boiling water. They were then seasoned, sealed, and placed in a pressure cooker for an hour or so. The well-stocked pantries and cellars of early East Texas homes stood in silent tribute to the dedication of hard-working housewives.

Jellies and jams were made from traditional fruits plus corncobs and butter bean hulls. They also made vinegar from fruits and beer from potatoes.

Pickling is a process of preserving foods with vinegar or brine. A variation of spices and seasonings results in spiced pickles, sour pickles, and sweet pickles.

Pickles were made from pumpkins, watermelons, zucchini, crab apples, and prunes.

To make a batch of East Texas chow chow, gather twelve and a half pounds of green tomatoes, eight large onions, ten green bell peppers, three tablespoons of salt, six chopped hot peppers, one quart of vinegar, a tablespoon of cinnamon, one tablespoon of allspice, a quarter-teaspoon of cloves, three tablespoons of mustard, several bay leaves, one and three-quarter cups of sugar, and a half-cup of horseradish.

Chop the tomatoes, onions, and green peppers. Mix them in a bowl and cover with the salt. Allow to stand overnight. Drain the mixture and add the hot peppers, vinegar, and spices tied in a cheesecloth bag. Bring the ingredients to a boil. Pack in clean jars. This recipe will make ten pints of chow chow.

To make traditional mincemeat, get four pounds of chopped lean beef, two pounds of chopped beef suet, a peck of sour apples (peeled, cored and sliced), three pounds of sugar, two quarts of cider, four pounds of seeded raisins, five pounds of currants, one and a half pounds of chopped citron, a half-pound of chopped dried orange peel, a half-pound of chopped dried lemon peel, one lemon (juice and rind), one tablespoon of cinnamon, one tablespoon of mace, one tablespoon of cloves, one teaspoon of pepper, one teaspoon of salt, two whole nutmegs (grated), one gallon of sour cherries and their juice, and two pounds of broken nut meat.

Slowly cook these ingredients for two hours, stirring them often. Fill sterilized jars and seal.

Pioneers ate pigs' feet—fried, boiled or pickled. The only drawback was the four hours required to prepare them. Many considered pigs' ears a more delicate dish. Ears were tender after only two and a half hours of cooking. Served along with the ears were sliced tart apples, fried until brown in a mixture of butter and pork drippings.

To smoke pork in a smokehouse, wrap the cuts in cheese-cloth to protect them from soot, run string or wire through the meat, and hang it from rafters. Hang hams with the hock downward in order to retain juices. Allow free circulation of smoke to all areas of the meat by spacing the pieces.

The ideal smoking temperature ranges between 110 and 120 degrees. Sawdust, chips, or small pieces of wood from apple, hickory, or oak make good fuel. The wood of all nut and fruit trees is suitable, as are corncobs. Never use resin-ous wood. Since smoke, not heat, is desired, keep the fire smoldering by lightly sprinkling it with water whenever it flares up.

The longer the smoking period, the better. During pro-longed smoking, the meat dries slowly and the smoke per-meates each piece. Quick smoking affects only the ham's exterior.

Hams may be smoked either for eight to ten hours or for a few weeks, depending on the quality desired. Generally hams are satisfactory in about five days, bacon in three.

Smoking time can be determined by color. Meat that is mahogany-colored all over, either light or dark in hue, may be removed from the smokehouse. The darker the meat, the longer it will keep.

Meat can be cured in two ways: by immersing the meat in brine, or by rubbing the meat with a salt mixture. Whichever method is used, each piece of meat must be rubbed with fine salt and allowed to drain, flesh side down, for six to twelve hours. Large pieces of meat need four days in the curing solu-tion per pound of pork. Smaller pieces require three days in the brine to each pound. When the meat is taken out, it should be soaked in clean water for thirty minutes.

Holding Water

Means of containing and dispensing water have long been a concern for people living away from the benefits of city services.

The simplest form of holding water for stock is the dirt tank or farm pond. The tank has an earthen dam across a draw or branch which impounds water during rainy periods for use when rain does not fall.

These little reservoirs were built using a slip or a Fresno scraper. The slip was a dirt scraper about two and a half feet square with sides some ten inches high and was pulled by a two mule team. The average slip could hold about four cubic feet of earth. There were handles on each side extending out behind, similar to those on an old-fashioned wheelbarrow. The operator controlled the bite of the slip into the earth by lowering and raising the handles.

The Fresno was much larger than a slip and required a three-horse team. Instead of two handles it had one long bar that came out from the back of the scraper. The bar had a drag rope attached to it to pull the Fresno back into scraping position after it had been dumped.

The mound of the dam was generally crescent-shaped, with the dirt piled a foot or more above the level the water would reach when the dam was full. Weeds and grass were encouraged on the dam to prevent washing.

More prevalent in some areas were watering troughs of various kinds. The standard wooden trough was constructed of heavy boards, two-by-twelve or wider. Six to eight feet long or more, the troughs were in a square-bottomed U shape. The ends were pieces of similar plank, fitted inside the U of the

body of the trough. No caulking was needed, because the wood swelled as soon as it was saturated with water and sealed all the cracks.

On some places, a series of troughs, each successive one at a lower level, was arranged in various pens and fed water from one trough to the next to provide water for livestock.

The troughs in smaller pigpens were of another design. Two boards, usually one-by-tens, were nailed in a V shape. They were generally five or six feet long. The ends were pieces of the same size boards nailed across the V. They served both to close the ends and to form braces to hold the V upright.

Smaller ones of the same design were used in chicken yards. Water was poured into both of these sorts of troughs from buckets.

Some farmers made troughs from metal or cement. Round, wooden troughs, usually of cypress, could be bought and were placed directly on the ground.

The most common water container before water was piped wherever it was needed was the ten- or twelve-quart galvanized bucket. The homemade oaken or cedar bucket was pretty rare. Sometimes enameled buckets were used for drinking water to avoid the metallic taste, as were enameled dippers. Homemade gourd dippers, however, were much more common. Dipper gourds, like most gourd plants, are easy to grow, and the dippers are easy to make. All that is needed is to cut away about a third of the side of the ball at the end of the gourd and then clean out the seeds and dried fibers on the inside.

Most pioneers used galvanized tubs for washing clothes and people.

One indispensable container was the iron washpot needed for boiling the dirt out of clothes, heating water for the washtub, and for scalding hogs, rendering lard, and making soap. A black washpot with a bleached-out poking stick sat in every farmer's yard not far from the woodpile.

The stone jug carried to the field by the farmer was bought in a store, but two additions he made were not. The cork or stopper was a piece of corncob, trimmed to fit tightly into the neck of the jug. The jug was covered with either tow sacking or cotton sacking stitched together with binder twine. The sacking was well dampened when the jug was filled, and each time the farmer took a drink he sloshed a little more water on it, so evaporation provided at least enough cooling to prevent the water from getting hot.

Underground cisterns containing rainwater provided water during dry times. The rainwater got into the cisterns through a series of drainpipes. When there was no cistern, rainwater was often caught in barrels or number-three washtubs placed under a valley in the roof. The soft rainwater was highly prized by the women for washing hair.

Personalized Country Ways
of Doing Things

Hattie Brunson knows about lye soap: "You used soap in the kitchen to wash the dishes, the baby's diapers (prettiest diapers you ever saw hung on a line). Lye soap makes things so white. There's enough lye in it, and that's what it takes to make white. We used it for bathin'. We bathed in a wash tub. Used lye soap for everything, even washing hair. You didn't have dandruff when you washed your hair in lye soap.

"To make lye soap, just follow directions on the can of lye. Take a gallon or a gallon and a half of water and put it in a big black pot that's on a fire. Put in a can of lye. When the water is hot, chunk in a gallon of cracklin's or whatever meat waste you had. Just let it boil and boil. Then take a teacup and dip some out into a saucer. If it congeals, it's ready. Take it out, cut it into chunks, and put it on a board to dry. It comes out kinda gold in color. Let it set overnight, then it'll be ready the next morning. Sometimes it just takes a few minutes to make a batch. Lye soap is made only when the moon is full."

Eugenia Godwin of Beckville says making butter is an art enjoyed by people who own and milk their own cows. "The milk has to be clabbered. It takes about fifteen hours with fine warm weather, but if the weather is not just right, it will not clabber that soon.

"Put the clabbered milk in the churn and make up-and-down movements with a dash, or stick with a propeller-looking device on the end. When the butter comes together, it is ready. Until then, it stays in little balls. Most of the time it will collect on the dash when it is ready.

"The dash has the form of a perfect cross on the end. It has a long handle, which makes it convenient for someone to sit or stand while churning.

"After the butter is made, it is scooped out of the churn and into a pan to be kneaded. The purpose of this is to get the milk out of the butter. After the kneading is done, the butter is placed in a butter mold. The mold holds a pound or half-pound of butter. When the butter comes out of the mold, it is in a neat little block ready to serve or refrigerate."

Gristmill

Leonard Beck, master miller, says gristmills were Saturday gathering places for farmers who lived in remote areas. One could get his corn ground into meal and catch up on the latest news.

Doril Wilkerson has a gristmill near Deadwood, Texas. It's next to her grocery store, which can't keep enough ground cornmeal on the shelves, because the demand is so great.

Leonard runs the mill and does about six bushels of cornmeal every Saturday. "People bring the corn to me on or off the cob. If it's on the cob, I start with the sheller to get the corn off. Then the corn is put in the hopper on top. It goes down through the grinder and the meal comes out the front.

"It's sifted through the screen on the hopper and it's all ready for the kitchen. I can make it coarse or fine."

Sunbonnets

The name is from the coarse medieval cloth called "bonnet," derived from the Hindu *banot,* from which early hats or hoods were made.

There are different styles of sunbonnets. Some are made with hoods divided into sections about two inches wide and six inches long. Into these sections you inserted little slats of cardboard, often cut out of cracker- or soapboxes. Before you washed the bonnet, the cardboard slats were removed.

In the early days, women had different bonnets for different things. Some were for work, some were for everyday, and some were Sunday-go-to-meeting bonnets.

They ranged from the very inexpensive and plain to those with ruffles, buttons, appliques, or laces. Women talked about bonnets at various meetings.

Bonnets are worn to protect the head from the heat and to protect neck and ears from the cold. Some women can't go outdoors bareheaded.

Some bonnets have short brims and are ruffled.

A. W. Smith appreciates the country life. "In early spring, poke salad was plentiful. Mother would parboil it for about fifteen minutes, then dip it out and rinse it in clean water, then boil it until it was tender. Then dip it out of the water and put it in a frying pan with some bacon drippings and cook it for a few minutes. Then scramble about four eggs in it.

"We also gathered wild lettuce and wild onions that grew along the creek banks in early spring.

"We loved fruits. One of the first things to ripen about the middle of May are dewberries. They're good to eat with cream and sugar and make excellent jellies.

"About this same time the mayhaws get ripe. They look like a miniature apple, about half an inch in diameter. They grow in river and bayou bottoms. We used to gather them by the tubful and sell them. They make good jelly.

"We also had an abundance of wild plums, both red and yellow, which ripen in June.

"Elderberries and blackberries make delicious eating, as do muscadine grapes, which grow wild along with the wild persimmons and huckleberries.

"Hickory nuts and black walnuts are delicious eating. We usually laid in a good supply. We sat around the fireplace on cold days and cracked nuts and picked them out of the shells.

"The chinquapin is a small, bushy tree that grows nuts encased in a thorny hull. When ripe, the outer hull cracks open and makes it easier to get the nut out. The kernel has a sweetish flavor. They get ripe in late summer.

"The bull nettle seed tastes like a brazil nut, takes patience and skill to collect without getting stung by the nettles.

"Rabbits and squirrels are best fried or smothered. You can make chili out of swamp rabbits (larger than a cottontail). Just mix a little fresh fat pork with it and ground it up for sausage.

"In late fall possums get fat on persimmons, blackhaws, and other foods. My dad would boil it until it was tender, take it out of the water, and place it in a big pan, like a roaster. He put a lot of candied yams around it and baked it until it was a golden brown. It was fat and greasy.

"I liked hunting the possum. For a light we took long strips of rich or fat pine about three feet long and the size of an ax handle. We split and splintered one end so it would burn. We carried these torches so we could see to get through the woods. This was before we owned a good gas lantern or flashlight.

"You had to be extra careful to avoid letting the hot tar drip on your hand. It really did stick and burn.

"We usually carried a pocketful of roasted peanuts with us to eat.

"Sometimes the dogs would tree a possum. If the tree was small, we cut it down. We always carried a good sharp ax with us. We hunted them for fun and sold the furs.

"We built bird traps for blackbirds. It would catch a dozen blackbirds at a time. We put an ear of corn in there, and when the birds came in to eat it, it tripped the trap and the box fell on the birds. We fried them, made bird stew or dumplings, or fixed them with dressing. The trap was preferable to a shotgun, to avoid eating birdshot.

"We caught fish using trotlines or hoop nets. I learned to knit fishnets when I was seventeen. We sold some of the fish for twenty-five cents a pound. We also caught hard- and softshell turtles, which tasted like brisket.

"Honey from bee trees also made good eating.

"Before refrigeration, we put a lard bucket full of milk with a lid on it on a rope and let it down in the well to keep it cool. We tied the rope so the bucket hung a little above the water.

"The bucket was a long, slender tin bucket about five inches in diameter and about twelve inches long. It had a ridge molded around it, down about four inches from the top, and a cup made to fit loosely in the top. It had a tight-fitting lid over the top of the bucket. Butter was placed in the cup on top and a gallon of milk in the bottom. These buckets are real collectors' items now.

"One place we lived we used water out of a spring. We had a box fixed so the water from the spring flowed through it and we would keep the milk and butter setting in the box with the cold water flowing around it.

"We kept some food in a screen-covered cabinet about two feet square, five and a half feet tall, with about three shelves in it. A full-length door was hinged on one side. The whole thing was covered with screen wire (copper, so it wouldn't rust).

"A flat pan made of galvanized sheet iron was set on top and filled with water. The pan was about three inches deep and the size of the top of the cabinet.

"Then we would get a piece of thin cloth like wallpaper canvas, large enough to drape around the whole cabinet and long enough to lie in a pan of water on top and reach below the bottom shelf. We would lay a small, flat rock on the cloth in the pan to hold it in place. The water would seep down the cloth, keeping it damp. The cooler was usually placed in an open hallway or on the porch in a shady spot. The air passing through this damp cloth kept the milk and butter and other foodstuff nice and cool. It also kept the flies away from it. This cooler worked on the same principle as evaporative air conditioners.

"We used to tan squirrel hides for boot- and shoestrings. Skin the squirrel, then put some ashes on the hair side of the skin. Roll the skin up and tie it with a string. Then place it in a bucket, lay a rock on it, and fill the bucket with water.

"Let it soak for five days and take it out, unroll it, and scrape off the hair. Then scrape the flesh side and hang it on the line to dry. It'll be stiff, so take some neatsfoot oil and oil the skin all over. Rub it in until the skin is soft and pliable.

"Then use your pocketknife to trim a narrow piece of hide, going round and round the outside of the skin."

Digging a Well

When he was a boy living just outside Canton, Hollie Brunson had to carry buckets of water from the spring down at the bottom of the hill up to the house. One day in 1938, his dad decided to dig a water well.

"I asked my dad where we would dig," says Hollie. "He pointed to a spot on the ground about thirty yards from the house and said, 'Right here.'"

Lyde Welch used to witch for water around Canton, but Hollie's dad thought he could find water on his own.

Hollie asked his father if he thought they would find water. The father replied, "There's gotta be water down there somewhere." They got the shovel and posthole digger and started digging.

They dug a round hole about four feet in diameter. One of them would be in the hole; the other would be on top with a bucket and rope. "While I was in the hole, Daddy would send the bucket down to me, I'd fill it up with dirt, and he'd pull it up."

When they got down to between thirty and thirty-five feet, a trickle of water started coming in. They called it a day and went to the house.

Hollie used to love to sit on the front porch swing with his dad, who smoked a pipeful of tobacco he grew on the place.

The next morning, the hole they dug the day before had about a foot of water in it. "We dipped that all out," says Hollie, "and went down about another eight feet. We really hit the water then. The water was coming in, so we had to get out. It was up to my knees and we couldn't dip it out fast enough. So we quit for the day."

The next morning, water in the hole was within fifteen feet of ground level. "We figured we hit a pretty good stream of water."

They built a rock wall about four feet tall around the top of the hole, put a brace with a pulley on it, got a rope, looped it through the pulley, and tied a bucket onto the rope so it could be raised and lowered into the well. On top of the well they built a wooden lid to keep leaves and other things from falling into it.

To get the water, they would lift the lid, lower the bucket into the well, let it fill up, then pull it back up, empty the water into a container, close the lid, and hang the bucket on a nail on the pulley brace.

Years later, they rocked the sides of the well. Eventually

they put a pump in the well and ran a water line into the house.

The family still went to the spring for drinking water, but used water from the well for washing. Hollie says the spring had the best-tasting water he's ever had.

"The spring was about three feet deep and had the clearest water I've seen," says Hollie. "The sand around it was snow white. It was pretty big. You could dip a bucket in it and never hit the sides or bottom."

He says when you washed clothes with the springwater, the clothes came out extremely white without using any bleach. "And we didn't have to use much soap. That water was very soft."

The spring was their refrigerator, too. They kept jars of milk in the spring because the water was cool. "My daddy and I used to love to drink cool buttermilk from that jar that had been in the spring."

They had no icebox. "The ice man would bring a fifty-pound block of ice and Daddy would wrap it up in some old tow sacks, blankets, and tarps. We'd put a nice clean cloth next to the ice so it wouldn't get the ice dirty. Then we'd keep that out on the porch with a washtub over it. The ice man came by twice a week. We used the ice only for drinking iced tea."

Hollie said neighbors told them the well he and his daddy dug wouldn't last very long, but it did. "Every once in a while when we'd have a dry spell, the well got low on water. Then a rain would come and the well filled up again."

Cooking on a Wood Stove

Doris McLaughlin was born and raised in Latexo, a small place in Houston County just outside Crockett. Her grandmother reared her, and Doris wanted to honor her in some way, so she wrote a book called *Cooking on a Wood Stove* and put some of her grandmother's recipes in the book.

"I started out cooking on a wood stove myself," says Doris. "When I was a young teenager at home, that's what we had. Actually, it's pretty easy to operate. First you put your wood in the stove and start a fire. You do your cooking on top of the wood stove, of course. If you want something to cook fast, you put in another stick of wood. If you want it to cook slower, you move your cooking utensil away from the main heat. We used to say move it to the back of the stove. Then it won't cook so fast."

Doris's stove was in the kitchen of the house. When her grandmother was young, the kitchen was in a separate building away from the house.

Doris called her grandmother Aunt Sally because that's what everybody called her in Latexo. "She was a midwife par excellence and an old-fashioned kind of nurse," says Doris. "She would leave home for two weeks at a time and go help someone who was sick. She was just always Aunt Sally, so that's what I called her."

Aunt Sally cooked with a pinch of this and a pinch of that. She never wrote down any of her recipes. "So you can imagine what a time I had trying to put these recipes down in any kind of form that someone could use," says Doris. "I remembered how I used to cook on a wood stove and I learned how to do it from my grandmother. So my recipes were actually her recipes. Even today I still follow her recipes."

Doris says her grandmother used to bake delicious sweet potatoes. "They'd be warm on the stove when we came home from school. Her fried chicken was superb, and so were her raisin and mincemeat pies. She used to make a molasses cake that was wonderful. And it would always sink in the middle. I have tried my best to re-create that, and mine will not sink in the middle.

"She could take Irish potatoes and make them about fifteen different ways and you would swear you were eating something different every time. She was not a real fancy cook, but it was good, wholesome, down-on-the-farm-type cooking. She always raised a garden and she canned, so we always had a lot of good stuff.

"Aunt Sally killed a hog every year, so there was always plenty of ham and pork chops. Her cornbread was outstanding, and the rolls she made were light and fluffy."

The kitchen table was the center of activity in the house. It was unusually long, with benches along the sides. The table was always covered with an oilcloth. Silverware was kept in a jar or bowl in the middle of the table.

"That table in my grandmother's house really meant something to me," says Doris. "In addition to serving meals on it, the table was also a place where surgery was performed. When my grandmother was about fifty years old, she climbed up on the table and had a hysterectomy. She told everybody if she didn't see them anymore, goodbye. They put her out with ether and operated on her by lamplight, and she came out all right. They got all the sheets in the house, scrubbed the walls down, and put the sheets on the walls, scrubbed the floor and table with lye soap that she made herself in her washpot, then operated on her."

Squirrel Hunting without Bullets

Gene Allen lives way out in the woods near Crockett. He is an extraordinary hunter and loves to tell about his adventures. In cold weather he wears camouflage fatigues every day. "I'm always ready to hunt," says Gene.

He is a roofer by profession. "When I'm not working, I'm hunting deer, hog, squirrel, or ducks."

Gene grew up near the place where he now lives. He was one of ten children. When he was about ten years old, he pulled enough cotton to buy a little .22 rifle. One Sunday afternoon, his daddy told Gene to go get his .22 that they were going to get a mess of squirrel for supper.

"We got the guns and the dogs, crossed the road, and walked down to the branch," says Gene. "The first squirrel a dog treed was in a real tall, slick pine on the side of a hill and the wind was blowing. I didn't have but eleven shells when I got over there, and I shot the tenth one before I got that squirrel.

"It kinda made my dad sore. He told me we ought to go back to the house, since I wasted all those shells. We started back up through the woods.

"We had three dogs with us, and each one of them treed a squirrel in a different tree. We had an old collie that treed by sight. He wouldn't trail one, but he would watch a squirrel and run him in the timber. I went over there and started clapping my hands and stomping around in the brush. The squirrel jumped out and the dog caught him.

"I went over to my dad and he was standing by a little post oak where one of our dogs had treed a squirrel. He got to beating on the side of the tree with his ax, and that squirrel jumped out and the dogs caught him. That gave us three squirrels. Daddy said, 'Let's see if we can get one more.'

"We went on to the top of the hill, where old Rex had a squirrel up in a sweet gum. My dad chopped the tree down, and the dogs and I were standing where it fell. But instead of the squirrel staying in the top of the tree, he came back down the trunk and crossed over that stump. Daddy was trying to hit him with that ax, and I chased it with a stick and the dogs were after him. That squirrel pulled out his tricks. He'd go between the dogs' legs, and I chased him 'til I was about give out. Finally he went up one of those big virgin pines, I mean one of those real tall ones with a trunk on it four foot through. The squirrel was tired, too, and he stopped on the side of that tree.

"My daddy was a good shot with a rock or a pine knot, and he picked up a pine knot and threw it at that squirrel and hit him right in the back of the head, and he dropped to the ground.

"We got one squirrel with ten bullets and three with no bullets," said Gene.

When he got home with the squirrels, they skinned them and had a good meal. "When you're skinning them, you put the young squirrels on one side and the older ones on the other side. The young ones are best fried like chicken, and you eat 'em with gravy and biscuits and ribbon cane syrup. The tough ones, you boil them, then roll them in flour and fry them. Or you can brown them like a roast, put them in a pressure cooker, and tenderize them. 'Course, you can make dumplings or squirrel stew or whatever you like the best."

Gene learned how to use a slingshot when he was a little boy. "That's what we hunted with. My brother got two pairs of pigeons one time and put them in our old log barn. Within two years we had about five hundred of them, and the barn got real nasty. My dad got aggravated with them, so we took our slingshots and spent about a week getting rid of all those pigeons."

Some East Texas Jokes and Stories

I met Drayton Speights the other day in the drugstore across the street from the courthouse at Hemphill. The half-dozen Hemphill residents I had become acquainted with over coffee all told me I needed to meet him. So when he came in (everybody comes into that drugstore at Hemphill) we made plans to get together later at his house.

His residence is one of those fun places you run across every once in a while. It is down a quiet, tree-covered lane and sits back off to itself. It has a long front porch that offers a splendid view of the nearby woods.

When we settled in to talk, I asked Drayton if he knew of any practical jokes. Sure enough, he did. He said during World War II there were sightings of flying saucers. So he had a mechanic make one, complete with batteries and old radio tubes. He put it in a narrow road a mile east of town so anyone who came by would see it. Sure enough, some old folks who had been out to play croquet noticed the contraption when they were returning home. They called the sheriff to come out and see about it.

Now, Hemphill is a small town, so when the sheriff gets a call about a flying saucer falling to earth, suddenly everybody in town knows about it. So a whole group of people went

out to investigate. The curious included the city's newspaper editor, who photographed the UFO and sent the story and picture to the Beaumont newspaper. The next morning the headlines read, "Flying Saucer Found Near Hemphill."

The story detailed how the county judge was afraid to touch the thing, so he shoveled it out of the roadway. Once back in town, a merchant said he wanted it to display in his store. Just everybody in Hemphill came by to see it and say things like, "I don't see how on earth the thing could fly." That prank was good for a couple of weeks.

Drayton once put out a story that a lion had escaped from the Dallas Zoo and was loose near the community of Brookeland, not far from Hemphill. Churchgoing folks down that way swore they saw it. Men said it chased their calves. Ladies were afraid to pick their blackberries. After a few days, Brookeland people thought it might be a joke of some kind.

Drayton says people would rather believe a big lie than the truth. "Tell a big yarn and folks go to wonderin' about how much truth is in it."

Drayton used to do business occasionally with a man who owned a little store near Hemphill. "He had a very complete line of merchandise," says Drayton, "all the way from coffee and snuff to coffins and whiskey. Every time he sold a quart of whiskey on the credit, he'd pour a quart of water in the barrel. During cold weather it got to where his whiskey would freeze it got so weak."

He used to have a fishing friend who drank a lot. One time he and Drayton had maneuvered their boat just a few yards from shore and his friend reached under his seat, got out a big bottle of whiskey, threw the top away, and handed the bottle to Drayton. "That's yours," the friend said and reached under his seat, got another bottle, opened it, and threw that top away.

That friend used to read lots of stories

in Western magazines. "He was a real storyteller," says Drayton. "He'd tell one of these stories and institute himself as the main character. He'd tell about going to West Texas or Colorado. He would tell about going to Japan if he'd had enough to drink. He'd tell you about traveling to the Orient on a steamship and would even name the boat and tell the whole story just like he read it. But he really wasn't a world traveler. His brother-in-law told me he had never been nowhere but to Orange and his folks had to send him money to get back home from there."

Growing Worms Is Serious Business

A few years ago, Ed Lovelace started a worm farm near Woodville. He bought $20,000 worth of worms and built a huge bed to hold them.

The bed was eight feet wide and longer than a football field.

He filled it with wood chips, rice hulls, and cow manure.

"We had to go to every ranch around there and fill up trailer load after trailer load of cow manure," says Ed. "We had to buy a mixer and mix all that stuff together in the proper proportions, then we put it in the bed."

Then Ed put the $20,000 worth of worms in the bed and you could hardly even tell they were in there. "Those worms didn't make a dent in that big worm bin."

Ed bought another $30,000 worth of worms and put them in the bed.

"All told, I had about $60,000 invested in the worms," says Ed. "And every time I turned around, my worms were leaving."

The worms were afraid of noise and light. And every time it stormed, there was trouble.

"The lightning would flash and the worms would head for the bushes. They'd come out over the sides of that bed and head into the grass and disappear forever."

Ed could just visualize all of his investment going into the ground.

"We had every light in the place turned onto that worm bed to try to drive the worms back in. All the wives and children and men were gathered out there with flashlights going through the grass grabbing up big hunks of worms and putting them back in the bed."

He put a sprinkling system in his worm bed and put a roof over it.

"Then spring came and the birds came. I'll tell you, they must have sent telegrams to every bird in America, because they all came to my worm place. They had a feast. All they had to do was fly down there and poke their bill in there and they'd come up with half a dozen worms. Fat birds, man, we had the fattest birds in the country."

Ed sent his worms to fishing camps by air. And the cargo handlers weren't too careful with the containers. Finally the airlines told Ed they wouldn't haul his worms anymore.

"If you put tens of thousands of worms in an airplane and they get out of the container and they crawl everywhere, no matter how the airline tries to clean that out, some of the worms have gotten away. They're gonna go through every crack they can find in that aircraft, trying to find a way of escape or getting to food or getting to water or something, and the first thing you know there were worms in the seats. So the passengers began complaining. This was another reason the airlines wouldn't carry the worms anymore."

School Lunch

Eddie Trapp teaches junior high school science at Cooper in northeast Texas. He grew up there. In addition to his teaching duties, he has coached and driven a school bus.

"I figured up one time and found out I had driven a school bus about ten times the distance around the world."

Eddie is a catfishing guide on Cooper Lake. He holds two lake records on blue cat and channel cat.

"The blue catfish record is twenty-four pounds. The lake is still young. Those fish will get a lot bigger than that. The channel cat record is a little over fifteen pounds."

When he's not working, he hunts or goes fishing.

"I take my camera with me and take slides of snakes, turtles and trees and show them to my students in class. I think it's important that kids learn what type of flora and fauna they're growing up with."

Eddie does some after-dinner speaking.

"I like to tell about goin' to school.

"Now, everybody has heard about having to walk ten miles to school, through the snow, barefooted and all that. But there's a new little twist on that I like to put in, and that is that it was uphill both ways."

He talks about tough times.

"Growing up, we didn't have much to eat, usually. Just what we grew in the garden. One year our garden didn't do too well. The only thing that grew was okra.

"We were too poor to fry it, so we had to boil it all the time.

"I had to carry boiled okra sandwiches to school every day for several weeks.

"I was so tired of those boiled okra sandwiches.

"I made up my mind one day that I was not gonna eat any more of those sandwiches, so I decided to accidentally get the wrong sack lunch.

"Just before lunchtime, I went into the little room where the lunches were kept and felt all those sacks. I felt one that was real heavy.

"I thought to myself, 'Boy, I'm gonna have a feast today!'

"I grabbed the wrong sack (accidentally, of course), stuck it under my coat, ran out on the

playground, hid behind some bushes on the corner of the playground, and thought I was really gonna have myself one good
meal. It was a big, heavy sack.

"Now, you gotta remember everybody had it pretty hard
back then. I looked all around to make sure nobody was
watching.

"I opened that sack and looked in there.

"It was a hammer and eight hickory nuts."

Surviving in the Woods

Milton Bullock and his wife, Faye, moved to the East Texas woods a few years ago. They had lived in Houston, where Milton worked for a large construction firm. He wore suits and ties and Gucci shoes on the job. Now he wears his Gucci shoes with his overalls.

Their place is just outside Maydelle. They had bought the land a few years back thinking they would have it as a retreat. They had even started building a small cabin on it. Milton's heart attack and a four-way bypass speeded their retreat to the woods. When they moved in, the cabin only had three walls completed. They spent several nights sleeping with rain pouring in the cabin.

Getting electricity was no small task. They had to bring it in from the highway a quarter of a mile away. Three days were required to cut trees so lines could be strung. There's a lot to learn living in the woods.

Milton and Faye don't go to extremes with this survival stuff. They don't eat bugs in their cereal. But they have roughed it. Milton drilled a water well, laid the water and sewer lines, and put in a septic tank. He even added that last wall to the house.

One evening, after they had been in the woods just about a week, Milton and Faye were eating supper by candlelight (that was all the light they had then) when their dog started barking at something in a tree. Every sound they could not definitely identify was scary to them. Milton grabbed a flashlight, but it wouldn't work. He went outside and in the bright moonlight noticed the outline of a cat without a tail perched in the tree. He thought, Bobcat, of course, and went inside and got his .38. He lined up the cat between him and the moon and fired. Got it. Turned out to be a yellow housecat with a red collar on it. Someone was minus a pet. Milton learned another lesson about living in the woods.

Once some neighbors gave Milton and Faye a bushel of tomatoes. They decided to make catsup. Milton attached a juicer to the kitchen table, and Faye began cramming tomatoes into it. The juice started spurting all over the kitchen walls, ceiling, and floor. When it came time to add water and cook the tomatoes, they hoisted a big pot up to their kitchen cookstove. The pot was so big it covered all four burners. The resulting heat from under that pot froze up the handles on the stove and they couldn't turn them off. They finally resorted to taking the mess outside and cooking it over a fire. It gave the catsup a smoked taste, anyway. They spent a couple of hours cleaning the tomato juice off the kitchen walls, ceiling, and floor. They ended up with a five-year supply of catsup. Milton figured that catsup cost about seven dollars and fifty cents a half-pint.

They decided to have a garden and some chickens. Milton built some fine hutches and bought some rabbits. Soon he had rabbits all over the place. Faye said, "Let's try eating one of those rabbits." Such simple words. Now, Milton had been watching the rabbits, and he discovered they were extremely nasty and their behavior was sometimes shocking. They ate their young. That nearly made Milton sick. Cautiously, he got his survival book and turned to the article on preparing rabbit for cooking. He tacked his book to a tree for easy reference. After killing his rabbit, he hung it up between two trees and tried to follow directions the book recommended for skinning the rabbit. He slit the rabbit down the front, then down the inside of its paws. The book said the hide should just slip off like a glove. It didn't. Milton worked exceptionally hard as he tried to separate the hide from the rabbit's body. He stretched it nearly all the way to the ground and it wouldn't come off. Finally he got a firm hold on the rabbit and stretched it out about ten feet. The whole thing came off from its hanging place and hit Milton right in the face. He really got sick this time. He struggled over to his survival book to see what he had done wrong. He had forgotten to remove the rabbit's head. The next day Milton called up a guy in Maydelle who was in the rabbit business and told him he could have all of Milton's rabbits and hutches if he just would come and get them.

Milton doesn't have any rabbits now. He's still learning how to live in the woods.

The Devil Made Texas

There is an old poem that has been researched and researched by Texas scholars for generations, and still its origin is uncertain. Some say the poem can apply to any area or state, but I don't think so.

On a recent CD released by the Gillette Brothers of Lovelady, Texas, Pip Gillette sings the poem. It's called "The Devil Made Texas" and goes like this:

O, the devil in hell,
they say he was chained,
and there for a thousand years he remained.
He neither complained, nor did he groan,
but decided to start up a hell of his own,
where he could torment the souls of men
without being shut in a prison pen.
So he asked the Lord if he had any sand
left over from the making of this great land.
Well, the Lord he said, "Yes, I've got plenty
    on hand
but it's way down south on the Rio Grande.
And to tell you the truth,
the stuff is so poor I doubt it will do for a hell
    anymore.
Well, the devil went down
and looked over the truck
and said if it came as a gift he was stuck,
for after he'd examined it careful and well,
he decided the place was too dry for a hell.
Well, the Lord, just to get the stuff off of his
    hands,
he promised the devil he'd water the lands,
for he had some old water that wasn't no
    use—
a regular bog hole that stunk like the deuce.
So the grant it was made, the deed it was
    given,

the Lord he returned to his place up in heaven.
The devil soon saw he had everything needed
to start up a hell, and so he proceeded.
He scattered tarantulas over the road,
put thorns on the cactus and horns on the toads.
He sprinkled the sand with millions of ants
so the man that sits down must wear soles on his
    pants.
He lengthened the horn of the Texas steer
and added an inch to the jackrabbit's ear.
He put water puppies in all of the lakes
and under the rocks he put rattlesnakes.
He hung thorns and brambles on all of the trees.
He mixed up the dust with chiggers and fleas.
The rattlesnake bites you, the scorpion stings,
the mosquito delights you by buzzing his wings.
The heat in the summer's a hundred and ten,
too cool for the devil and too hot for men.
And all who remained in the climate soon bore

stings, bites, and scratches and blisters galore.
He quickened the buck of the bronco steed
and poisoned the feet of the centipede.
The wild boar roams in the black chaparral—
it's a hell of a place that we've got for a hell.
He planted red peppers beside all the brooks;
the Mexicans use them in all that they cook.
Just dine with a Texican and you will shout,
"I've got hell on the inside as well as the out."

Pip's singing is heard on the CD "The Gillette Brothers'
Lone Star Trail."

Move Over, Dan Quayle

John Foster has a parking meter in front of his office in
downtown Henderson. It is the only parking meter in town. It
has a small sign with the words "free parking" printed on it.

"Most of the time nobody parks there, because they think
they'll have to pay," says John. "They don't see the little sign
saying they can park free. Lots of people pull in there and start
fumbling for change. That's what's funny. Seeing these ladies
looking in their purses trying to find a nickel."

He says people will try to put money in it, discover the
coins won't go, then they'll see the sign and laugh. "A few
times, some people have become irritated."

Parking meters were removed in downtown Henderson
about fifteen years ago. The previous owner of this building
didn't let them take this one, however. When John bought the
building, he just kept it there.

"It's real easy to tell people where my office is. I tell them
it's right behind the parking meter."

John grew up in Tulia. He had a paper route, and on one
of his collecting trips a customer told him the money was out
there where he usually found his paper. "He had put his
monthly fee for the paper in a jar that was in a ditch way in
front of his house."

John had trouble with spelling in Tulia. He was in a county-wide spelling bee when he was in the fifth grade.

"My mama was so proud of me. There was supposed to be four students from Kress, four from Happy and four from Tulia, in the contest. But the students from Kress and Happy didn't show up. There were four students in the contest, and I finished fourth."

He misspelled the word potato.

"I spelled it t-a-t-e-r. One of the judges jumped up and told me I had missed it because I put an 'e' in it. I guess that sort of qualified me for the office of vice president of the United States."

John joins some of his friends every morning for coffee in a drugstore near his office. The room where they meet has a barber chair in it, and the one who tells the best joke or story gets to sit in the chair. John sits there frequently. "Those morning meetings are very educational."

He got a call from a telephone marketer the other day wanting to know if John was "a small business man." He told them no, he weighed 270 pounds.

John makes a living as a free-lance court reporter.

"It's a very interesting profession. You learn lots of things and really get a broad-based education about life, I think. I was looking at some records the other day and found out I had reported 7,000 hearings in sixteen years as the official district court reporter. Some of them were very short, like a name change that takes five minutes. I reported over 3,200 divorce cases. I sort of got to be an authority on the subject. I figured out what causes divorce. It's marriage."

Cooking Stew

Stew has been a main staple in East Texans' diet forever. Perhaps the most famous stew is found in Hopkins County. "Hopkins County stew was made from what was available," says Henry Sartain of Sulphur Springs. "The basics were corn, potatoes, and tomatoes. You had to have a little meat in there, and it didn't matter what kind. You'd shoot a squirrel and have squirrel stew. You could kill your neighbor's chicken or a buzzard or anything you could get. Water was the main ingredient, and there was plenty of it. You never ran out of stew until the well ran dry."

Hopkins County has one of the oldest cook-off competitions in the state. "It's a pretty big deal. We usually have about a hundred people entered in the competition," says Bill Elliott of the Sulphur Springs Chamber of Commerce.

The modern-day cook-off has become the biggest annual event in Sulphur Springs, drawing as many as 10,000 people. It takes place the third Saturday in September every year on the grounds of the civic center. The cook-off has its roots in history.

"Hopkins County stew originated back in the twenties and thirties at the end of the school year in the rural school communities spread throughout the county," says Elliott. "At the end of school in the spring, all the students and their parents came in and had a big celebration."

Each school had its own event. Some had baseball games or stage plays or horse races, but they all had stew. People brought different ingredients

and put them in a big pot of boiling water. When the stew was ready, everybody had at least one helping.

"I'd say we had eighty school districts in Hopkins County at that time," says Astor McKeever, who attended some of the early end-of-school events when he was a boy. "There is no real recipe for Hopkins County stew. It's just what you have

on hand at the time. In the early days, most of the meat was squirrel. It was the most available. We didn't have many chickens or beef to use for that purpose, but we could go out into the woods and shoot a squirrel right quick. The fellows would have a chopping block and they'd chop it up, then cook it bone and all. The meat would come off the bone and they'd throw the bones out."

Elliott says many families get together at the annual event and have a reunion. "It has really become a significant thing for the community and for people who attend on a regular basis."

Astor McKeever says the early Hopkins County stew events became famous. "You'd go all over Texas, maybe even all over the South, and if you mentioned you were from Hopkins county, people would say, 'Oh, Hopkins County stew.'"

The cook-off has a "super stew" category open exclusively to previous champions. Charley Charles Jr. and his wife, Mary, have won the "super bowl" half a dozen times. "We just have some magic ingredients," says Mary. "We use the exact amounts of ingredients every time," echoes Charley. "We have eleven different spices in our stew."

Henry Sartain is famous for making the hottest stew in Hopkins County. "I love them Palo Pinto peppers," says Henry. "In fact I love all types of peppers, and we put 'em all in our stew."

The Big Thicket

When spring comes to the Big Thicket, mud gets hub deep, the sweet gums and loblollies stand erect, and Carolina wrens sing proudly.

The Big Thicket today is only a remnant of the dark wilderness that once spread across more than three million acres of East Texas. It was a region of tall trees and swamps that was home to panthers, bears, wolves, moonshiners, and desperadoes.

The thicket used to have so many pigeons that residents could hear the tree branches snap from the weight of the flocks.

The thicket was rich in oil and timber, and that brought entrepreneurs who took most of the thicket away. The sound of the pumpjack and chainsaw drowned out the birdsong.

To protect the thicket from being destroyed by industry, Congress set aside 100,000 acres as a national preserve.

The thicket is bounded by Segno on the north, Sour Lake on the south, Batson on the west, and Kountze on the east. Little Rock, Votaw, Bragg, and Saratoga are communities within the thicket.

Pigs are considered noble beasts in the thicket. They are allowed to run free to fatten on acorns, then are rounded up and butchered when food runs short. Sometimes hunters bring in the hogs alive for further fattening before slaughter.

The boars have tusks sharp as razors and make a formidable prey. The wild hogs are hunted with dogs that have stamina, courage, and sensitive noses. They always find their way back home no matter how far they chase pigs in the woods.

The thicket is called a biological crossroads of North America, overlapped by Appalachian and southern forests, flora and fauna of the West, and varieties indigenous to Mexican subtropics.

Briar patches and palmettos abound. Sometimes the way is blocked and you get scratched. Cactus grows right beside moss. Magnolia and beech trees tower over yellow jasmine plants.

In this natural laboratory, there are forty species of orchids, twenty-six different ferns, and four of the country's six types of carnivorous plants that gobble up insects and lizards.

The thicket has a wet climate, with fog and flooding quite common. Things rot quickly in the thicket. Metal rusts, and wood is dissolved and devoured by moisture and insects.

Red-tailed hawks patrol the uplands, and wood ducks squeal from the dark sloughs. Otter and beaver are plentiful. The long, melancholy howl of a wolf can be heard on still nights.

The earliest residents of the thicket were fugitive slaves and outlaws. Much of that independent spirit carries over to the people who live in the thicket now.

To them, rows of young pines planted by the paper companies are an abomination. They know how to take care of the game, the timber, and the fish in the streams.

Thicket people can survive on squirrel stew and fried rabbit. Many of the older residents bought their first pair of shoes for their wedding day at age eighteen. They have a deep and strange love for the land where they live.

Belief in the supernatural abounds. There are legends about buried gold, balls of fire, and panthers that sound like screaming women.

Names

East Texans love names. Names of people, places, nicknames. It doesn't matter. Hardly a day goes by that I don't hear of a name I've never heard before.

One elementary school class in Bryan, Texas, has students named Orangejello, (pronounced O-RON-jilo), Lemonjello (pronounced Le-MON-jilo), Aquanetta, Kleenexia Tissuetta, Quinetta, and Ebony.

So when I mentioned to the teacher of the class that I had information about some of the most popular names of babies recently born in Texas, she was only mildly interested. "We're not into just your common, everyday, ordinary names around here," she replied.

Apparently some mothers name their babies for items found right in the hospital room. Kleenexia Tissuetta, indeed.

Elsdon C. Smith, a Chicago attorney who founded the American Name Society in 1951, lists twelve principles for choosing a name for a baby:

1. It should harmonize with the family name.

2. It should be easily spelled.

3. It should be easily pronounced.

4. It should carry with it only pleasant nicknames or pet forms.

5. It should not evoke unpleasant connotations or associations.

6. It should fit the nationality of the bearer.

7. It should have a pleasant meaning.

8. It should produce initials with a good meaning or pattern.

9. It should not create confusion with the namesake.

10. It should clearly identify the bearer.

11. It should not be odd or unusual as to evoke constant comment.

12. It should designate the sex clearly.

Dr. Fred Tarpley, the Texas name expert, has done some research and has compiled a list of the most popular names of babies born to all Texas residents in recent years.

MALE	FEMALE
1. Christopher	Ashley
2. Michael	Jessica
3. Joshua	Amanda
4. Matthew	Brittany
5. David	Sarah
6. John	Stephanie
7. Justin	Samantha
8. James	Elizabeth
9. Daniel	Lauren
10. Jonathan	Jennifer

The ten most popular names for white baby boys recently born in Texas were: Michael, Christopher, Matthew, Joshua, James, John, Justin, William, Jacob, and Cody. White girls were named Ashley, Sarah, Brittany, Lauren, Amanda, Taylor, Shelby, Chelsea, Elizabeth, and Courtney.

Most black baby boys born during the same period in Texas were named Christopher, Joshua, Michael, Brandon, Anthony, James, Jordan, Robert, Darius, and Xavier. Black girls were named Jasmine, Ashley, Brittany, Jessica, Taylor, Amber, Danielle, Alexis, Briana, and Courtney.

The most popular names for Hispanic Texas boys were Jose, Juan, Luis, Jesus, Daniel, Michael, David, Christopher, Jonathan, and Joshua. Hispanic parents named their girls Jessica, Ashley, Stephanie, Maria, Amanda, Samantha, Jennifer, Vanessa, Crystal, and Elizabeth.

Dr. Tarpley says the new listing indicates the influence of soap operas and the frequent use of names starting with the letter J. He cannot explain why so many baby girls were named Taylor.

The names of Texas communities are fascinating. I've been to the East Texas villages of Bump, Nose, Two Egg, and Hot. Dr. Tarpley says the name Salem crops up occasionally in East Texas. It's short for Jerusalem.

The Naming of Cut and Shoot

The community of Cut and Shoot is located in the northeastern part of Montgomery County. It had its unusual beginning and acquired its peculiar name in July of 1912.

The Missionary Baptist, Hardshell Baptist, and Methodist citizens of the community went together and built a combination church and schoolhouse. They erected the structure with the understanding that all three denominations could hold services there. The building was called "the community house."

In July of 1912, a preacher named Stamps, of the Apostolic belief, appeared in the community. Some of the local brethren invited him to hold a meeting at the community house.

Now, it was rumored about Reverend Stamps that he occasionally visited saloons and went dancing. This upset some people, and the issue of whether Stamps should get to use the community house divided the residents of the community into two sides: those who thought the community house should be used for all denominations, and those who thought it was to be used only by the three groups which built the facility.

The Apostolics declared their intentions to have the meeting, and the other side claimed the meeting would not be held. On the morning of July 21, 1912, the group wanting to hear the preacher gathered at the community house. They had come in their wagons and buggies and brought their lunches with the intention of staying and having all-day preaching and dinner on the ground. Under their wagon seats they had their guns and knives rolled up in quilts.

They found the doors of the building locked.

Soon the anti-Apostolic group arrived and declared that

the lock was jammed and nobody could enter the building. An argument broke out, and both factions grabbed their guns and knives.

While the accusations flew back and forth, an eight-year-old boy of one of the men became frightened at the disturbance and said, "I'm scared. I'm going to cut around the corner and shoot through the bushes in a minute."

Thus the name of Cut and Shoot was coined.

Photo taken by Tumbleweed Smith

There was no actual cutting or shooting that day. But the arguments continued. As a compromise, the meeting was held under shade trees.

The next day, both sides appeared in Conroe, the county seat, and charged each other with disturbing the peace, assault, and the use of obscene language.

Both elements in the case received fines. This dispute was carried on between two of the men for over a year, each bringing charges against the other on the smallest pretense.

In one such trial, a male witness was asked by the judge where the fuss had taken place. He replied, "I guess you would call it the place where they had the cutting-and-shooting scrape." This was the first indication that the new community might be called Cut and Shoot.

On April 5, 1969, an election was held to incorporate the town of Cut and Shoot. On May 17, a mayor, five councilmen, and a town marshal were elected. The population of Cut and Shoot today is approximately 300. Residents are extremely proud of their community and pass out bumper stickers promoting Cut and Shoot.

One person who popularized Cut and Shoot in the fifties was Roy Harris, a boxer who called Cut and Shoot home. Roy's daddy was his trainer and wore overalls and a coonskin cap and carried a long rifle to the boxing matches.

Roy's daddy trained several boxers in the community. To keep the boys off the ropes, he strung barbed wire around the practice ring.

A Couple of Hunting Stories

Cecil Ford says in the twenties there were plenty of bob-cats, squirrels, quail, and 'coons, and a lot of small game. "There were few panthers. Many of the quail have gone, but there are still a lot of squirrels and 'coons along the thick brushy creeks.

"Nearly all the fox hunting is gone, because people started in with ranching, and it brought in the wolves, and the wolves kept the foxes out. The wolves came along to get the baby calves.

"There used to be no limit on the number of quail that you killed. You could kill twenty-two or twenty-three out of a box of shells with a good bird-dog. It was no problem to kill sixty-five or seventy quail in an afternoon. There was no limit on squirrels, either. If you took an old .22 single shotgun, you could kill twenty to twenty-five in one day with a good squir-rel dog."

Marvin Wolfe has spent some time in the East Texas woods. "There used to be quite a few panthers here. I re-member some men went hunting down at Cave Springs Branch. The dog struck on something and ran it a little while, barking and baying. When the men got to where the dogs were, they had a panther on a drifted log out in the water. One of the dogs swam out to the panther, and the panther jumped off the drift onto the dog, pulling him under the drift to drown him. One of the men told the other that he was going to get his dog. They waded out to where they went under. One man reached down in the water and caught hold of the panther's hind legs. When he pulled him up, the other man stuck a knife in his ribs and killed him. Those men were determined to get their dog, because their dogs were their money and food.

"We used to have a lot of doves a long time ago, because people didn't hunt them much. Lots of people wouldn't kill them, because they were a sacred bird.

"When I was growing up, people went out and killed deer when they wanted to. There was no closed season. Many of the deer were killed out, and many left when people started clearing land.

"When my daddy first came here there were black bear, but there was no closed season. I could remember one time a man and his wife had killed two hogs and had them hanging in the smokehouse. That night when they went to lock the smokehouse door, they saw that the door was open. They eased up to the door and shined the light from a pine splinter in the smokehouse. The man saw it was a bear eating on some meat. He picked up a club, went in the smokehouse, and killed the bear. The man dressed the bear and hung him in the smokehouse with the hogs. The man had to kill the bear, because if he didn't have the meat, it would have been a hard winter for them."

Marion L. Davis Sr. says armadillos came to East Texas from South Texas about 1936 and were called "gravediggers." "People used to trap 'coons and save their furs. You could get a pretty high price for them. Sometimes $15 to $16 for one. The skins were made into hats and coats and sent back here to sell.

"People used to trap minks. You might get $30 a hide. But minks were scarce then. There are plenty now."

Mules

Mules are the offspring of the male donkey (jackass or jack) and a female horse (mare). Sometimes a female donkey (jenny) is matched with a male horse (stallion). This results in a hinny, an animal inferior to the mule.

Mules are sterile but exhibit the combination of vigor and hardiness from both parent species.

Mules were the most popular farm animal in East Texas and were used for a great variety of work, from log hauling to pulling a wagon. The mule population dropped off drastically when the tractor came along.

Buck Rushing says mules sold for different prices. "A

good pair would run $400. Three- and four-year-old mules brought more than the older ones. During the depression, the government bought mules for people who didn't have the money. They called it the rehabilitation program.

"They had the three-day test: The people would take some mules and work them for three days. If they didn't like them, they could bring them back. If they liked them, they just kept them."

Raybon Ford says you had to teach the mules how you wanted them to work. "One thing was to show them which side of the wagon you want them to work on. If you had a pair of mules working, you'd have one work on the left side and one on the right side. That's for working with a wagon or plowing or pulling logs. Most of the time, if you swap sides with them you can't get anything out of them. You break him to the side you want him on and keep him there the rest of his life. Make him work right there.

"You bought mules at sale barns in Carthage. They had plenty of mules—you just picked out one you liked. They were young, never been harnessed up, never been broke. You bought him, brought him home, and put him with an older mule. That older mule would help him. He'd help him behave and learn.

"A mule works better than a horse. He's made for work. A horse is not as good. Some are, but most of them are more sensitive than a mule. A jack is his daddy, and he's stubborn. You cross him with a horse and you get a mule. A mule is easier to handle 'cause he's got his daddy's and mama's traits. They are a lot smarter than people give them credit for.

"I'd rather have a mule than my tractor. I think you can plow better with a mule. My daddy and I logged with them for years, loading logs all over this country. Our mules learned to work well for us. As they worked in the woods, they learned to turn around and come right back to you. They learned the work and they liked it. Their main trouble is overeating. Some will eat all night.

"You hardly ever saw a mule in the woods kick from any kind of excitement other than bumblebees or yellow jackets stinging him. He'll kick then, and I don't blame him. I've gotten four head of mules into yellow jackets in the river bottom. They were dragging a log, and I went off into a slough. The log got into a drift, and that drift had a yellow jacket nest in it. The log got hung and the mules couldn't pull it. The yellow jackets were stinging them, and I had one gray mule that tried to lay down. I was trying to get them loose so I could get them and me out of there. They were stinging me just as bad as they were stinging the mules. I couldn't leave the mules. I had to whip the gray one to keep it from laying down. If he'd laid down in their nest, they'd have stung him to death. I was finally able to get slack enough to undo them and got us all away.

"When we bought a new mule, we put him with the smartest mule on the place so he could learn. If I came to a bridge, the young mule might be afraid of it. That old mule would walk right over it. The young one might try to push him off, but that old one would hold him on to keep him on the bridge. Or he might meet a car and sit back and be scared. But that old mule would walk on like nothing was happening. It would be a day or two and that new mule would walk on across with the old one 'cause he knew it wouldn't hurt him. That's the best way to train one. So you can see there's a whole lot of work in training a mule.

"Mules built all the roads in East Texas. They did the work that bulldozers do now. They're made for work. I like to see them earn their feed. If you don't work him, he gets rowdy. As long as you keep him in the harness six days a week, you get good work every time. If you give him a week's rest, he'll try your patience.

"Mules will learn their names fast. If you call him, he'll pick up his ears and listen for it. They'll know their names and they'll look for you when you call them."

Rudolph Marshall has had some bad experiences with mules. "You have to keep an eye on a mule or he'll kick you, and I've been kicked by them. In plowing, a mule has a steadier pull than a horse. A mule's got sense, plenty of it.

"When you want him to go to the right you say 'Gee.'

When you want him to go left you tell him 'Haw.' When I was a boy we had a dinner bell. My mother would ring that bell at eleven o'clock. We had a little mule, it was a mouse-colored mule. And she'd hear that dinner bell ring. If we were headed away from the house, that mule walks just real slow. But when you got to the end of the row and turned back to go towards the house, you better get ready to walk, because that mule was gonna walk your legs off coming back. She knew that was dinnertime just as well as you. She knew that dinner bell was quitting time.

"We fed our mules corn and oats. They had all they could eat. We wanted them to be in good shape so they were able to work good. If you treated a mule right, feed them good and use good harness, they'd work for you. Back then mules were more plentiful than horses."

Sybil Scott had a good mule. "He worked really well and minded well. We were so proud of our mule.

"Once we noticed our pears were missing and we could not find any on the ground. So I looked out one day and that mule had got himself up against this tree. He shook that tree and down came those pears. He ate every one of them. He was real nice about it. He did not shake down any more than he could eat. Every day he would go out there and get him some more pears."

V. B. Newman says the average mule lives to be about twenty or twenty-five years old. "Some have been known to live thirty-five years. My daddy had one live to be thirty-two years old."

Joe Snelson says the mule has got a short memory and a thick hide. "You can teach him something today and he will forget it by tomorrow. After he once gets it set in his mind he'll be all right."

Joe McLeroy has worked mules. "A mule is more dangerous to work than a horse until you get him plumb gentle, because he will kick you. Then you can't trust his heels. He'll kick you for the fun of it.

"I always fed my mule three times a day, just like I ate myself."

Marvin Wolfe says you can pet a horse, but don't pet a

mule. "Mules can stand more heat and have more endurance than a horse. They eat less and cost less to keep than a horse. Mules are stronger than horses.

"When you buy a mule, get one that is tight, made like a barrel and broad between the breast. You want a nice smooth-cut head on them. Get a mule that was broad across the forehead. They're more intelligent than straight-headed mules. One that's broad across the breast and long from his hip to his hock is strong. In other words, you don't want to have what they called 'too much light' under one. His body is too high off the ground.

"If a man had light land, like sand, you could get you a little mule that weighed six or seven hundred pounds and work him good. If you had bottom land, heavy land, you would get bigger mules. In the early days, people used steers, but after more sawmills came into the country and things began to pick up, they went to using mules."

A. W. Smith knows how to talk to mules. He says "Get up" means go forward. "Whoa" means stop.

Copeland Pass used to have a good fox-trotting mule. "He rode just like a saddle horse. Usually a mule was more determined than a horse. And a mule would bring more money than a horse back when I was growin' up.

"We worked 'em on a lot of different things. When we made syrup, I used to feed the cane in the mill which squeezed the juice out. And we powered that mill by a mule who went round and round. I've worked four mules on a wagon at a time hauling logs. It took four mules for an eight-wheel log wagon.

"When I was a boy, the mule was the only way to get around. We hitched them up and went to church in wagons and to town. When I got married and built my house, I took my mule and used him to move my stove to that house.

"One time I hitched two mules to the wagon to go get some switch cane. We had a baby at the time. One of the mules was a young mule. He had never been worked. We started back home and he wanted to run away. I pulled on the

line and it broke. When it broke, I pulled the other way and liked to turn the wagon over. I had to walk the line up in front of him to stop him. And my baby was in that wagon."

Gus Davis has a two-acre garden he tends to with his mule named Mandy. "She's just a family mule. I've got a boy over there, Eldon, that uses it. Cecil Britton, my son-in-law, uses it, too.

"This is the third crop I've made with Mandy. Mandy is old, I don't know how old she is, maybe forty. She's been around for a long time. But she'd pass for sixteen or eighteen years old. She can eat corn off the cob. Mandy is a smart work mule. You can talk to her and she'll listen. She'll do what you say to do.

"If you were starting off to train a new mule now, well, it would take a year or so to get one thoroughly trained. It takes that long for them to understand your language."

Zed Wooten likes to start out with a two-year-old mule. "If you take a six- or seven-year-old, they're just too old to start. I like a mule that weighs a thousand pounds, something that's big enough. If you take one of the smaller ones to plow, it's like he's straining too much to pull that plow."

Callie Mae Davis used to have a mule named Babe. "She taught me how to plow instead of me teaching her. We planted cotton and corn. I was about eight years old and Babe was six when I started plowing with her. Babe was always as fat as a butterball. She would go right down the row, and all I would have to do was hold on to the handles and the planter.

"We had another mule named Coley that Papa always plowed. I would hitch old Babe and Coley to the wagon every Sunday and we would go to church. That wagon would be loaded down with young folks going to church.

"I could ride old Babe to the field and back bareback. I plowed in the field and hauled water with her. You could plow old Babe without a line. All you would have to do was talk to her."

Harry Truman, in his book *Plain Speaking,* wrote, "Plowing a field with a mule is the most satisfying thing a man can do. And at the end of the day, looking over what you've done, you can feel a real sense of accomplishment, and that's a very rare thing."

Fauntine Welch recalls what her family did after working with mules all day. "When we finished our work in the field it would be nearly dark. Everyone had a job to do. Someone milked the cows, and the wood had to be brought in for the fireplace and cookstove. Water had to be drew from the well. And we put it in a bucket. While the children were doing their work, supper was being fixed. We had a long table with benches on the sides with chairs at each end. And my father sat at one end and my mother at the other end. The children sat on the benches. The blessing was said by my father. When supper was over, it was time for my father to read the Bible. We had to sit quiet while he read, and he would stop and explain it to us. Then he would pray and it was time for bed. We had to get up at four o'clock. But on Saturday and Sunday we did not. We went to church and visited with our neighbors. We would have company nearly every Saturday night. We would sit on the floor and they would tell us ghost stories. We had a happy home and a good life to live."

Pioneer East Texas Architecture

East Texas is a world of barns and fences and worn wood-grain. Frances "Ab" Abernethy of Nacogdoches, the guru of the Texas Folklore Society, learned about pioneer homes from the old ones that were crippled over to one side with their ribs showing and their blank eyes staring. They were houses unadulterated, with all their sins and blemishes apparent, showing how the maker put them together in the beginning. Sometimes the chinking still showed the marks of fingers and palms, and old worried boards revealed bent square nails with the cuss words still on them.

When the old structures finally go, the old chimney stands for a while like a tombstone over the place till time and vines drag it into the dust from whence it came.

East Texas log barns were being built in the thirties and forties, and they will be there till somebody pushes them over.

The old barns are usually kept where land and property are handed down. People that belong to an area keep the objects of their families' and their culture's past. New people clean out for a fresh start.

The old folks have planted the vines from which we gather grapes, and the stock is still strong and the fruit is sweet.

Early buildings in East Texas were traditional. Families took the materials at hand—logs, rocks, sometimes the very earth itself—and built with those materials whatever it took to survive. The methods used to shape the logs or shingles were those learned from forefathers. The buildings satisfied not only the immediate needs for which they were built, but also satisfied what the eye has been conditioned by culture to see as beautiful.

Texas is particularly suited for the invasion of immigrants from all directions. From the northeast came the Scotch-Irish. Across the southern states came the English, Scots, and Irish

Photo taken by Tumbleweed Smith

who had earlier left Virginia and the Carolinas. Into Galveston and Indianola came Germanic and Slavic people from Europe. And from the south across the Rio Grande came the Mexicans. Each group brought its own styles and methods of building, and each adapted the styles to the material at hand and began building to keep off the rain and to cope with the raw, wild, new land called East Texas.

Building materials were easy to come by in East Texas, where tall, straight pines grew, ready for hacking and hewing.

Most of the homes were built in a hurry. The pioneers planned to do better as soon as possible. Early houses were primitive, because the builders had neither the skills nor the time to do better. The East Texas countryside is filled with structures that went from housing people to housing animals or hay. Many of the early buildings were built with inexperienced hands and flexible brains that were able to accomplish the task at hand by figuring out step by step just what to do. And they couldn't just run down to the hardware store for a piece of equipment or material. They used what was near.

The structures they built served them well and stood the test of time. They kept them in good repair.

When a pioneer built a log cabin in the East Texas woods, he started by sawing down trees and making notched logs. He then fitted them together, filling in the spaces between logs with "cats," wads of mud mixed with grass. Cats were also used to make chimneys.

Most of the early East Texas homes were square. A porch was added for additional space and the opportunity to do some serious "porch-settin'." In the evenings, families gathered on the porch to talk over the day's activities, wave to neighbors who might be passing by, or observe the stars.

The house became a symbol of stability, determination, and courage. To carve out an existence in the East Texas woods, starting a farm and a new life represented an opportunity that had been only a dream for a long time in the minds of the pioneers.

The method of building depended on the tools at hand. A good ax, either double-bit or with a driving head, was the first necessity for the new Texan building in the timber regions.

After deciding on a location for the house, trees were cut, particularly those which were at least fourteen feet high and ten or twelve inches in diameter.

A strong woodsman equipped with a good sharp ax can cut fifteen or twenty such trees in a single day. Once felled, the logs are notched, then dragged by chains and a team of oxen to the building site.

Early East Texas homes were built about four feet off the ground. This was accomplished with logs seven feet long. Three feet would be buried in the ground; the remaining four feet served as building blocks for the sills and joists on which the floor was laid. The raising of a house four feet above the ground was necessary for protection against insects, especially ants.

The roof was constructed with gables on either end and logs spaced between them to hold the shingles, which were made of cedar or elm. To make shingles, the round trunks were sawed into blocks three feet in length, then split into small planks of an inch and a half to two inches thick.

The height of the house was usually ten to twelve feet high, with plenty of room for a sleeping loft. In warm areas, the kitchen was built outside the house.

The farm complex included the house, barns, and all the outbuildings necessary for the family to maintain its self-sufficiency. Settlers who brought livestock with them usually built a barn first, then a house. Those who arrived with just a wagonload of possessions put a house at the top of the building priority list. The settler then built his barn or crib to protect his corn, tools, and plows. Chicken houses, pigpens, cow lots, and gardens were added and fenced to keep animals and crops separated.

As the farmer prospered, he built water tanks, milkhouses, and stock troughs. He built a long furnace with a chimney to hold the long pan for making syrup. He dug a cellar to store canned items and built a smokehouse where he could cure and keep his meat.

Open-sided hay barns were built to dry out hay. They were sixteen by twenty feet, made of peeled pine logs. The cost to make one was about $150, most of that for nails and roof tin. The pine trees were selected, cut and trimmed, then moved to the site and peeled. The barn was then built, using trusses, braces, and supporting logs. There were no walls.

The placing of the buildings was for the greatest efficiency, with the milkhouse and smokehouse near enough for the wife to use easily, and the outhouse, hog pens, and chicken house far enough away to dilute their characteristic aromas. All the structures were situated so the least movement got the most work done.

Trade Tokens

Lumber companies used trade tokens. Instead of paying their employees with real money, they paid them in tokens that would say "good in trade" at their store or commissary. Employees of the mill would have to trade and do business at the company store.

Some had the number of hours worked and the value: one-quarter day's work was worth 25 cents. One hour's work was 10 cents. That meant the day was ten hours long.

"Twelve and a half cents in trade" was a valuable token used in saloons, good for one free drink. That came from the Spanish influence, two bits being worth a quarter.

Some were given away at general stores when people bought a large order of goods. The tokens would be worth a dollar.

Some were good for a shave at barbershops, a loaf of bread at food stores, or a free soda at the drugstore.

If a person sold eggs or butter, he would be given a token good for the value of the merchandise brought in.

Tokens were aluminum, brass, copper, wood, or paper. Some were round or scalloped or square.

Some tokens are worth $50 to collectors. They were in use from 1880 to 1930.

Fun at Any Price

Poverty was prevalent at the turn of the century. One family lived in a cave and existed primarily on stewed bull nettle nuts. But somehow, no matter what the sacrifice, settlers showed up at entertainment events.

Toby shows, featuring a clown with a red wig, were performed on a stage under a tent. Between the singing and dancing, candy hawkers would sell saltwater taffy with a prize in every box.

Films would be shown on a screen in a tent from a rickety projector.

Slide shows were big events. Admission was a dime, and slides were shown at school. The visiting couple would put a bed sheet on the blackboard and project painted glass slides onto it. The slides would be projected from a wooden box with a carbide lamp in the back of it. The slides were pictures of Abraham Lincoln, animals, and American cities.

Another form of entertainment was hypnosis. A man might hypnotize his wife, stick a hat pin in her face, and ask someone from the audience to remove it. Then he would put

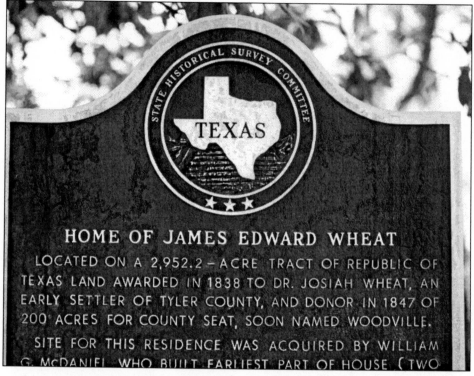

HOME OF JAMES EDWARD WHEAT

LOCATED ON A 2,952.2 – ACRE TRACT OF REPUBLIC OF TEXAS LAND AWARDED IN 1838 TO DR. JOSIAH WHEAT, AN EARLY SETTLER OF TYLER COUNTY, AND DONOR IN 1847 OF 200 ACRES FOR COUNTY SEAT, SOON NAMED WOODVILLE.

SITE FOR THIS RESIDENCE WAS ACQUIRED BY WILLIAM G. McDANIEL WHO BUILT EARLIEST PART OF HOUSE (TWO

her head and heels on the backs of chairs and ask someone to stand on her.

Jugglers, acrobats, magicians, and high-wire artists came to town with the Mollie Bailey Circus. She would set up a tent on a vacant lot and put on the show. A cage of monkeys provided more entertainment. Other animals were wolves, a bobcat, and a cage of rabbits.

The old swimming hole was another diversion. Usually a rope hanging from an overhanging limb provided the chance to swing and splash.

Young boys got BB guns when they were ten years old or so. They considered it their finest instrument, because it could kill squirrels and provide meat for the table.

A favorite pastime for boys was bird thrashing. Birds would roost in brush that had been cleared off acreage. Boys poked in the brush, the birds flew out, and the boys would hit them with the leafy parts of small plum trees they had plucked from the ground. Then they would take the feathers off the birds, build a fire, and eat them. They carried salt with them for seasoning.

Country Miscellany

During times when lots of family members were around and there weren't enough seats at the dinner table, adults would eat first, then the table would be cleared and the kids would eat. The little ones would usually stand by their parents and watch them eat. The older folks would feel intimidated and eat quickly.

Iced tea was served in big jars, already sweetened. The silverware was kept on the table at all times in a big canning jar, with the handles to the bottom of the jar.

The tablecloth was an oilcloth with a bright pattern. The seats were benches except for at the end of the table, where the man of the house sat in his cane-bottom chair.

Light came from coal oil lamps that were turned on at dusk. The musky smell of kerosene wafted through the house when they were first lighted. Residents usually didn't keep them burning very brightly, because they would use more fuel that way.

Newly married couples would be serenaded by young boys in the community who played French harps, beat on tin cans or dishpans, and rang cowbells.

Quilts/dyes: Get rich red clay, mix with water, put quilt lining in the water, and it comes out red. Bark from red oak, sweet gum, or maple trees makes purple dyes.

Luella Wooten: "I went to a little country school. A one-room building. We had to walk about a mile and a half, and it was woods all the way. We went to school the three months after Christmas. I went about six years. I could learn everything in all those books except one. I never could see any sense in arithmetic. I could never learn that. I sat there and cried many a time because of arithmetic.

"Every Saturday morning we carried the corn to have it ground. We would shuck it Friday night and have it ready for the mill Saturday morning. We shucked it by hand for a long time, but finally we got a corn sheller.

"We lived on a crossroads and everyone that came by, my husband asked them to have supper with us. We always had enough though it was vegetables out of our garden and chicken. I had lots of chickens and we'd have fresh pork. We never killed much beef. Beef peddlers would come by with that. They would come at different times in the month. We'd buy just enough to eat right then, because we had a whole bunch of folks to feed."

D. D. Chadwick: "Me and my daddy went down there in the field one day and we came along on some birds and they flew into the woods. I climbed in a briar patch to make a bird fly up. The bird flew up and came back over me. I just shot straight up and reached out and caught him before he hit the ground. My daddy said, 'I bet you can't do that no more.'"

The Smokehouse

Felton Marsh: "We slaughter the hogs in cold, fair weather, but not freezing. The hogs are cut up, and hams, bacon, roast, and stuff like that go to the smokehouse. I salt it down while the animal heat is still in it and let it stay down twenty-one days. You put the meat in a good, large wooden box and cover it up with salt.

"After twenty-one days, look at the salt on top. If the meat is not spoiled, the salt will crack and settle down in the box. If any of the meat is spoiled, the salt will bulge or raise up. The meat taints around the bone sometimes if the weather is not just right when you salt it down.

"Then you take the meat and wash it in borax water and wash all the salt off of it. We start the smoking process in the winter when it's fair and cool. Don't wait until the spring.

"Hang up the meat in the smokehouse and start your

hickory smoke under it. Burn the hickory wood in a number-three washtub four feet below the meat. If the smokehouse had a dirt floor, I guess the fire would be started on the dirt. I usually smoke the meat for about two weeks. The last few times you add wood to the fire, I use sassafras, which gives the meat an extra-good flavor.

"After the meat is done smoking, I have a sure way to store it so it stays good. You get a wide-mouth jug and stuff the meat in there. Then you pour hot lard in it and let it harden up good. Then you turn the jug upside down. It keeps it from getting tainted, just like canning. I have eaten meat that was two years old.

"I build my smokehouse as tight as possible. That way, the meat stays cooler. I use the smokehouse to raise small chickens in before I start smoking the meat. I clean it out good and spray it good first."

Syrup Making

John Brooks: "Cane was grown and made into syrup for use on biscuits at breakfast. The syrup was also used on most any food.

"Seed cane has to be cut and put down in the field in a bed covered with dirt before the frost hits, otherwise it will ruin the cane. It will sour and wouldn't come up.

"In February or early March, take the cane out to the beds and plant it in rows. As the cane sprouts and comes up, we cultivate the cane through all the summer into the fall of the year. Around November, or anytime before the frost, cut the cane, strip it out, and carry it to the mill, where it'll be pressed and the juice made into syrup.

"The juice is run through the mill where it's ground, and the juice comes out of that. Then it is strained into a barrel and into an evaporator. Some people call it a syrup pan. That pan is sitting on a furnace. The juice comes in the pan at one end and it goes through a series of baffles, circulates all the way down to the other end fourteen feet away. By the time it gets to the other end, you can tell if it's done by looking at the bubbles. Then it's strained into another pot, then put into buckets.

"We made 100 to 125 gallons of syrup a day. When I was a kid we used to buy one-gallon buckets for four cents apiece.

"Lots of older people would come and drink the juice. Just get a jar of it, carry it home with them, and put it in their ice-box. They would drink it as long as it lasted, then come back and get another one. It makes awfully good syrup. It's got all that sugar. Most of the syrup we buy now has artificial flavoring in it."

THE SYRUP MILL
by J. P. Hightower

When I was a lad, one bright sunny day
I was out in the yard real busy at play.

When my dad said, "Son, come go with me,
There's something over yonder I want you to see."
We got in the buggy, the horse struck a jog,
The dust clouds behind us really started to fog.
We drove for an hour, or maybe it was two.
The places we passed were all kinda new.
We turned off the road through a gate in the fence.
I'd never been there before and haven't been since.
We went around a bend and down a long hill,
And there in the valley stood an old syrup mill.
The grinding mill was something to see.
It stood upon posts that were taller than me.
A big long log was what made it go.
One end was high and the other end low.
A mule was hitched to the end near the ground.
He just kept on going, just around and around.
The rollers kept turning at a good steady pace.
As the juice was squeezed out it would squirt in your face.
The feeder at the mill said to me with a grin,
"Come over here, boy, you can stick some in.
Now, don't get too close, it will get you," he said.
"And duck under that beam, or you'll get a bumped head."
I put in some cane and went around to see.
The stalks came out mashed flat as could be.
The juice drained down into a big tank.
He dipped up a cup and gave me a drink.
It was strong and sweet and not strained too well.
I didn't like it too much, but I wasn't gonna tell.
The feeder man called to the other side,
"Hang on to that beam, boy, and take you a ride."
I rode a few rounds and then turned her loose,
For another man came for a bucket of juice.
I greeted him and then he went by
And poured it in a keg way up high.
He poured four buckets of juice in that keg,
Then reached over and turned a little peg.
The juice squirted out in a little round stream
Into the syrup pan all covered with steam.
The pan sat up about as high as Dad's belt.

With all of that fire I thought it would surely melt.
One end was open where they threw in the wood.
The man threw some sticks in to keep it going good.
The smoke bellowed out at the smokestack end
That high in the sky, it was caught and carried by the wind.
With all that fire and smoke I was really surprised.
The smoke and steam all went away, 'stid a gettin' in your
    eyes.
The syrup pan was long and wide and really built to stay.
It would hold a barrel of juice, with partitions all the way.
The partitions didn't reach across, not clean from side to
    side.
An opening was left for juice to run, about four inches wide.
One opening on the right side, the next one on the left.
They said the way they had it fixed, the juice ran by itself.
His left hand held a stirring tool, a skimmer in the right.
Back and forth they pushed the juice, from early morn till
    night.
They cooked the juice all the way, down every little trough.
All the scum came to the top, they quickly skimmed it off.
A jar sat down at the other end, under a little spout.
The cooker man, he turned a spigot and let hot syrup run
    out.
It was bright and clear and looked like honey,
The way it bubbled and foamed, to me was funny.
"It's got to be good," the cooker man said.
Then he gave me a bite on a piece of bread.
When the jar got full, here came a man.
He pushed back the strainer and set down a can.
It was hot when he dipped it and filled up the pail.
Then he set it out plumb ready for sale.
Dad bought two buckets and paid the man's price.
They shook hands and he told him it had been real nice.
"I wanted the boy to see how this is done.
I think he'll remember, for he really had fun."
That's been many years, I remember it still.
That bite that he gave me, still hot from the mill.
It was delicious for breakfast with butter and bread.
"It's got to be good," that's what the man said.

Turkey Hunter

Edgar Bradford is not modest about his turkey-hunting ability. "I've probably killed more turkeys in Texas than anyone else," he says.

Edgar worked at the post office thirty years. When he retired, he was postmaster. Now he's a guide and takes people on turkey hunts.

The annual spring turkey-hunting season is from the April 6 to the May 5. Some flocks of wild turkeys have more than 200 birds in them.

"Some people say turkey hunting is hard," says Edgar, "but it's easy for me. I got five turkeys with one shot once. A bunch of them were pecking on some grain and I got two of them in my sights. The bullet must have ricocheted or something, because when the smoke cleared, five gobblers were jerking around."

Edgar has dozens of turkey-hunting stories, and he's eager to share them with people who have an interest in them.

Edgar gets his hunters out early.

"If the sun comes up at 7:00, I like to be in position by 5:30," says Edgar. "Then I'll do a little calling just to let them know I'm around. They gobble back at me while they're still roosting."

For cover, Edgar prefers a small bush. He gets behind it and is still and quiet. The only sound he makes is with his caller, a hollow turkey-wing bone. He has used the same one for a dozen years. "You have to dig the bone marrow out of it or it'll stink." He sucks on the caller to make the sound of a hen.

Edgar has been in some turkey-calling competitions and has not done well. "Those city folks have names for the sounds turkeys make. But a hen just yelps. And a gobbler just gobbles. They oughta have live turkeys at these calling events. Then we'd see who can call up a turkey."

Edgar has challenged some of his hunters who use mouth

calls or cedar boxes, or drag a nail across a rock. "There was this one guy who had a caller he put in his mouth. When we spotted a turkey, he started calling with it. That ol' gobbler just looked up for a moment, then went right on with what he was doing. When I called with my wing bone, he came on over."

Edgar has called up a turkey to within three feet of him. "I'm good, but I'm no match for the real thing. I've had dozens of gobblers leave me when they heard a real turkey hen."

Edgar's callers are about four inches long and open on

both ends. He keeps one with him constantly. He lost one two years ago when he pulled his car keys out of his pocket. He found it the other day in his yard and was elated. "I don't know how I kept from running over it with my lawn mower." Callers really mean a lot to Edgar.

When he was young, his family ate a lot of wild turkey. "I didn't have a lot to do, so I'd go out and just listen to those turkeys. I heard the hens yelp till they got a gobbler to come see them. That's the sound I try to imitate today. Some people say I yelp too much. But that's the way a hen does it. She hardly stops until she gets her gobbler."

His father and older brothers all used wing-bone callers, so he does, too. "I try to get my hunters to within twenty-five yards of a turkey," says Edgar. "You have to shoot them in the neck so you won't ruin the breast, which is the best part of the bird to eat."

At seventy-eight years of age, Edgar's favorite thing to do is hunt turkeys. "I really get a kick out of it. And when someone I'm guiding tries real hard to get a bird and succeeds, then I feel good."

Death Customs

Sarah Youngblood: "Bells rang out the announcement that someone had died. When a person was buried, the head was toward the west. Close friends and relatives would sit up with the body, sometimes two or three nights in a row. Sometimes they put half-dollars over the eyes to keep them shut. Women wore black dresses.

"They were buried fast because there was no embalming. If someone died today, they would be buried tomorrow.

"Generally, while friends and relatives stayed with the body, others built a coffin.

"Some people were simply buried without a preacher or sermon, which seems sad. But most had a preached sermon."

Robin Hooper: "There is a man in the Timpson cemetery that is buried crossways with the other people. He went crossways with the rest of the people all his life, so they buried him that way."

Mrs. Mildred Beheler: "Coffins were made of one-by-twelve pine known as boxing plank. The inside was padded with cotton and lined with soft, white, silky material. A small pillow was placed at the head. Around the top edge and hanging inside was white lace, and over this on the top edge was one-inch satin ribbon. The inside of the lid was covered with the same material.

"The outside of the coffin was covered with the best grade of white, gray, or black sateen. White was used for babies and young people. Gray and black were used for the older ones.

"When a request was made for a coffin to be built, the measurement of the deceased was brought so the coffin was made to fit. The measurement was usually taken on a piece of cane fishing pole. Material was bought, and men came to help.

"Some coffin makers were never paid for their work. They never expected to be paid.

"The corpse was carried to the church in a two-horse or two-mule wagon by close friends of the family. A buggy was sometimes used if the deceased was a baby. The procession was a long line of wagons, buggies, surreys, and horseback riders.

"Homegrown flowers, if any were in season, were used. Friends dug and covered the grave.

"My grandmother always had a Civil War sword hanging over the head of her bed. It had hung there for years and never made any attempt to fall off the wall. It fell on the day she died."

Ellen Starkey: "One time I was walking down the path from a friend's house and a white horse appeared in front of me on the trail. The next night my husband died, and I figured this was an omen of his death."

Teresa Ritter: "When a shooting star starts, it is a sign of death. When a person is on a dying bed and calls a loved one's name that is already dead, they are fixing to die."

Mable Clark: "I was riding in a wagon down an old road

and a fireball rolled across in front of me, not over twenty feet away. Then it rolled off in the woods. Three times this happened. Right then my father died in the living room at home. We didn't have much of a mourning period, because it was right in crop time and the crop had to be harvested."

Mrs. Billie Robinson: "A sign of death is if you dream of a wedding, you will hear of a death. And after someone in the family dies, the clock will stop. Another sign of death is if you

hear three knocks on the door, you will hear of a death in the family."

Herman Venson: "When I was young, I can remember that it rained three days in a row. On the third day when the rain had stopped, Pa and I went outside. We looked up at the sky to see if it might rain again that night. Well, when we looked up at the sky, we saw three doves. My pa's face turned sort of black, which it always did when he got mad or was afraid of something. He looked at me and kind of mumbled something about something terrible going to happen tonight. I didn't quite understand what he was talking about right then.

"When we went outside, my mother saw how he was looking. She asked kind of weak like, 'What in the good Lord's name is wrong?' Pa just looked at her and said kind of weakly that something terrible and black was going to happen tonight. Ma asked him why he thought so. He said that for one thing, it had rained for three days in a row. When he had gone outside to see if there was any chance of it raining again the coming night, he had seen three doves flying around. Ma and Pa just looked at each other for a while, then we heard the tolling of the church bells. We sat there listening and counting the bells. Usually they rang the age of the person who had died. The bell had rung thirty-two times when we heard a knock at the door. Pa jumped up and ran over to he door to answer it. There was a man at the door who was about out of breath. He looked at Pa and told him that something had happened. Pa told him to come in. The man sat down, looked over at Pa, and told him kind of slowly that Pa's brother had died. He was thirty-two years old.

"Pa sat there for a little while. Then he got up and went to the door. When he got to the door, he turned around and told Ma that he was going on over to his brother's house to help get his brother ready. He wanted Ma and me to wait until morning to come and bring some food with us. When we got there the next morning, they had cleaned out the parlor. My uncle was on one side of the room and there were chairs placed all around the room. My uncle must have known that death was coming after him, because the week before he had gone down to the general store and bought him a casket for five dollars.

"I was trying to find me a mirror to comb my hair in, but couldn't find one. I asked Pa where one was. He said that they had been taken down and put up. I asked him why and he said that if you saw your reflection in the mirror after someone in your family had died, you would be the next one to die.

"I went back in the parlor to see my uncle and he had pennies over his eyelids. Pa said that was to keep his eyes from opening. That evening they buried him with his feet facing east. They took him to the cemetery in a wagon that was draped in black. We mourned his death for two weeks."

Mrs. A. E. Arnold: "When a prominent person died, we would sometimes get out of school to attend the funeral."

Mrs. Irene Essery: "When someone died, they were bathed and laid out on the bed, or they used a board until they could stretch them out on a bed. They called it a cooling board."

Bobby Reider: "A cat was not allowed in the house at any time that the corpse was in the house. The belief was that a cat would eat the corpse's eyeballs out.

"The coffin was loaded in a wagon, then a sheet was placed over the coffin with a quilt placed over the sheet. Two men usually rode in the wagon seat, and usually someone sat in a chair beside the coffin. The people would ride to the cemetery in wagons and on horseback. Four men lowered the coffin into the grave with ropes. Just before the corpse was lowered in the grave, the lid was nailed on the coffin."

Mrs. Faye Humber: "People believed that if an owl perched on or sat on top of your house at night and hooted or screeched, there would be a death in the family within twenty-four hours. Still others believed if you swivel a cane-bottom chair or rocker around, tilted to the side, there would be a death or critical illness within twelve hours. We always got rid of a hen that crowed, because this also meant death within the immediate family."

Epitaphs

An English writer by the name of Puttenham described the purpose of epitaphs as follows:

"An epitaph is but a kind of epigram applied to the report of the dead person's estate and degree, or of his other good and bad parts, to his commendation or reproach; and is an inscription such as a man may commodiously write or engrave upon a tombe in few verses, pithie, quicks and sententious, for the passer-by to peruse and judge upon without any long tarriance."

East Texas cemeteries, like those in the Panola County communities of Snap, Long Branch, Mt. Bethel, Mt. Olive, Macedonia, and Corinth, express the feelings of East Texans toward deceased family members.

Tombstones above children's graves reveal these inscriptions:

> He was too good, too gentle and fair
> to dwell in this cold world of ours.

> How much of light, how much of joy
> is buried with our darling boy.

> The soul of a child is the loveliest flower
> that grows in the garden of God.

> Sleep on, sweet babe and take thy rest.
> God called thee home.
> He thought it best.

Gone from our home but not
from our hearts.

A sunbeam from the world has vanished.

She was the sunshine of our home.

Budded on earth to bloom in heaven.

He is not dead but sleepeth.
Tis not the whole of life to live,
nor all of death to die.

I am not afraid to meet my God, friends.
How is it with you?

Some graves indicate the occupants are getting a well-deserved rest:

Having finished life's duties,
she now sweetly rests.
I have finished my work which
Thou gavest me to do.
Life's race well run
Life's work well done
Life's crown well won
Now comes rest.
His life our precious heritage.

Some epitaphs describe one's occupation or accomplishments:

Ordained Baptist minister 1896

He stands in the unbroken line of
patriots who have dared to die that
freedom might live.

Some comments on gravestones are short and to the point, while others express strong emotions:

Here lies the mortal remains of. . . .

We trust our loss will be His gain
and that with Christ he is gone to reign.

My darling one has gone before to
greet me on the golden shore.
It was hard indeed to part with thee,
But Christ's strong arms supported me.

My love goes with you and my
soul awaits to join you.

Farewell my wife and children all
from you a father Christ does call.

To know her was to love her.
The beautiful life she lived will
ever linger in the hearts of those
who love her.
Grace was on all her steps,
heaven in her every gesture, divinity and love.

Dearest, thou heart from us flown
to the regions far above.
We to thee erect this stone.
Consecrated by our love.

She was too good and gentle to live in this cold world.

An honest man's the noblest work of God.
His spirit smiles from that bright shore, and softly whispers,
"Weep no more."

Spook Sounds in the Woods

Phoebe Armstrong of Woodville recalls the dog days of
August as the time when dogs go mad, snakes go blind, creek
water gets stagnant, and birds don't sing. She has put down
some of her growing-up experiences in a book titled, *From the
Forks of Turkey Creek.*

She tells me trick-or-treat hadn't yet been invented when
she was growing up in the twenties. On Halloween boys pulled
pranks that mostly amounted to nothing more than minor mis-
chief such as turning over outhouses (they checked to make
sure they were empty). And of course there was ticktacking.

Ticktacking was handed down from father to son. It was only practiced late at night when sensible people were asleep. One end of a stout cord was tied to the screen wire of a window. The other end was threaded through a hole punched in the bottom of a tin can, then knotted around a stick. When the string was pulled taut, someone rubbed resin up and down the string.

It made the most eerie caterwauling you ever heard. And it could be heard a mile away. Even bedcovers piled high over your head couldn't blot out the noise.

Some guys used a rawhide string attached to a nail keg to get the ugly, scary sound. Every youngster who heard it knew that all the screaming banshees in the world were gathered right outside their window and were coming after them with blood in their eyes.

Most Halloweens years ago started with a street dance or party. Phoebe recalls one special Halloween dance that occurred during the horse-and-buggy days.

About sundown on October 31, a street was roped off in downtown Woodville and fiddlers began gathering and tuning their instruments. Soon the dust was flying as couples danced.

There was a combination hardware and feed store nearby owned by Mr. C. M. Davis. He enjoyed providing good benches for old-timers to sit on in front of his store. He built a concrete porch just for that purpose and put an awning over it. He kept the area clean. On the west end of the porch, Mr. Davis displayed the latest wagon on the market. It was brand new and shiny. Its bed and spring seat were sparkling green. Its metal wheels were painted red, as were the wagon's body and tongue. It was a thing of beauty, the envy of every farmer in the county. It was Mr. Davis's finest merchandise.

The wagon was there in all its magnificence when the evening started. When darkness began to fall, boys started slipping away, one by one. Soon, kerosene lanterns appeared around the area of the wagon. The fiddlers played while the girls danced halfheartedly with one another, anxious for the boys to return.

The boys came back within a short time and danced until

the fiddlers got tired. As the crowd left for the evening, some snickers were heard.

As you may have heard, news travels fast in small towns. The next morning when the store opened, more people than usual had gathered downtown. Men in little clumps whittled and swapped yarns.

When Mr. Davis arrived to open his store, he noticed his precious wagon was missing. He ran to where the wagon had been, walked back and forth along the porch, then searched around the entire building. He was about to panic when the crowd decided to let him in on the joke.

On the roof of his building sat his precious wagon, completely assembled. After a good laugh and congratulating themselves on pulling off a successful prank, the town boys brought down the wagon piece by piece and re-assembled it in its original location.

Mr. Davis checked on his wagon several times that day.

Remnants of the Past

"Used to, when highways were new, you could drive down and see old stuff on the side of the highway. That's all gone now. They've dressed everything up and took the old stuff away like they're ashamed of it. Well, they shouldn't have been. But these days, to see the old stuff, you've got to get on dirt roads."

Woodrow Foster lives along a dirt road in Shelby County. He has spent most of his life as an artist and is dedicated to painting East Texas.

"Now, I have seen a certain place year after year, pass right by it without thinking. Then one day it'll hit me and I think that I ought to paint that. So I do. Up to that time, it never made an impression on me."

He has no favorite subjects. He'll notice something he wants to paint, make a pencil sketch of it, then paint it. "I get the essence of a place with my sketch. Any certain quality I want to portray I have to remember."

He never uses a camera.

"You work for an effect. It's something you feel at that time. If it's a certain light or time of day, it doesn't stay there over three or four minutes and it's gone. And a camera, by the time you get everything hooked up, that effect is gone."

He paints nostalgia.

"About all that's left of our old life is just remnants. You'll see an old rundown gate or something or a barn, and you'll realize how rare they are, the kind I do. They're going fast and they're getting farther apart.

"What I put in my pictures may appear dim, but that's the beauty of it. It's something that's left alone and forgotten. Usually nature and age soften things."

He says nature is important to an artist.

"I think that's why I'm lucky to live in the country. I can study it firsthand any time I please. But a city artist is handicapped. If you want to be a good painter, you've got to study nature. Even if you're an abstract artist, you've still got to study nature. It gives you the ideas and puts that life there that you just can't get from any other source."

Woodrow Foster creates about 150 watercolors and 5 or 6 oils a year. His subject for one of his pieces was an old shelf on the side of a modest wooden home. On the shelf were all the essentials: a bucket of water with a gourd dipper in it for drinking, an aged cup with a well-used bar of lye soap in it, a bowl for washing hands and face, a broken mirror, and a rag that was once a towel.

He says that in his rural paintings, his subjects have to be something that strikes him as being interesting. He is inspired by fleeting scenes that might one day be significant.

All his work is based on images from Shelby, Rusk, Panola, Nacogdoches, Sabine, and San Augustine counties.

"If I get the right feeling about something, I'll paint it."

He usually paints something within a month after he sees it. "You can't put it off too long or you'll forget it."

Woodrow Foster feels he is painting old East Texas before it is all gone.

Games and Parties

Youngsters growing up on East Texas farms were talented at picking cotton, hoeing corn, milking cows, and other chores. Their parents and grandparents made sure they learned how to play, too. Social events were arranged for the boys and girls to get to know each other.

Games such as Go in and out the Window, Spin the Bottle, Post Office, Letters, Drop the Handkerchief, and Thimble were among the favorites. They danced to the "Cotton-Eyed Joe," "Put Your Little Foot," and "Hokie Pokie." They sang "Old McDonald Had a Farm," "Around the Mulberry Bush," and "Skip, Skip, Skip to My Lou."

Rules for the game of Thimble are simple. The kids form a circle, holding their hands behind their backs. Someone goes around and drops the thimble in someone's hand. Whoever guesses where it is gets to hide the thimble.

The game of Snap is similar. You choose a partner and dance around the circle until you touch someone, who becomes your new partner. Boys and girls take turns choosing the new partner.

Hide and Go Seek was (and still is) a popular game for children. Whoever is "it" closes his eyes and counts out loud to 100. Then he starts looking for the people who went to hide. Whoever is found first is "it" in the next game.

Jacks, Tic-Tac-Toe, and Questions and Answers were popular indoor games long ago in East Texas. So was Musical Chairs, the game played with one more person than chairs. When the music stops, everyone sits down in a chair. The person left standing is out of the game. Another chair is then removed, and the game is played until only one person is seated. That person is the winner.

Dominoes, 42, Checkers, and Chinese Checkers were played frequently in East Texas.

So were marbles.

Sometimes boys got into trouble for playing "keeps" with neighboring youngsters. Their mothers and daddies worked hard for the money they spent buying marbles for their kids and they didn't want them gambling away all their marbles.

The "taw" is the thumping marble, the one you shoot with. The others are called "ring marbles." You place the ring marbles in the playing area to set up your game. The marbles were usually made of stone. To see who went first, the players tossed their taws to see who got closest to the center of the square. Then they'd take turns.

One marble game, called Tennessee, was played in a four- or six-foot square. We'd put nine marbles in there, one on each corner, one in the center of each side, and one in the middle. The one who got the most marbles won the game.

You had to knock at least five of the nine out of the square. Your first shot would be from about six feet away; then you'd shoot from where your taw landed. Sometimes we played partners. If the other team hit your marble, you gave him them ring marble.

Another marble game was Seven Up. In a little two-foot square, you'd put a marble in each corner and one in the middle. You'd have to win seven games to call it "Seven Up." You stood ten or fifteen feet away, and if you hit the middle marble and knocked it out of the square, you got a game. If you didn't hit the center marble out of the square on your first shot, you had to try to hit all five out of the square. If your taw stayed in the square after a shot, you were "dead" or "fat" and were out of the game.

Sometimes marbles were played on a diamond-shaped field. Players shot at marbles inside the diamond from ten feet away. The diamond was ten inches long and five inches wide in the center. You'd draw a line about eight feet back and made the first shot from the line. The rest of the game was shot from outside the diamond.

Sometimes players poked holes in the ground and tried to get their marbles in the holes. The holes would be in a line nine or ten feet apart.

Players sometimes traded marbles. The marbles were kept in a special place, usually in a cigar box or leather pouch.

Mumble Peg was a popular game boys played with pocket-knives. Open the long blade halfway and the short blade all the way, and flip the knife toward the ground. If it falls with the big blade sticking in the ground, it counts twenty-five points. If it falls with the little blade sticking in the ground, it counts fifty.

The loser has to eat a match stem that's been driven into the ground.

Another version: Make a little peg about two inches long and stick it in the ground. Then players get out their knives and open the big blade, and each player gets three tries to hit the peg. Keep taking turns until the entire peg is driven into the ground. The person after the one who drives it into the ground has to pull out the peg with his teeth. It makes for some rooting by the loser, who ends up with a dirty face.

Blind Man's Bluff is played by blindfolding a person and heading him off in some direction. If he touches you, you are blindfolded and do the chasing. In East Texas, if the "blind man" was someone the players didn't like, they led him to the

edge of the porch and he would fall down and break an arm.
That usually put a stop to parties for a while.

Hayrides were usually in the fall after the hay crop was
in. A wagon would be piled with hay, and kids would climb
aboard and the wagon would take off. Usually the driver "got
lost" so the group would have to disembark, build a fire, and
get all warm before taking off again. Amazingly, the driver
would get his bearings and head home.

Making candy from sorghum or cane syrup was popular
in the fall. The syrup would be boiled down, cooled, pulled
until it was hard, then rolled on a table and cut into strips.
Sometimes we parched peanuts and made peanut candy.

Hopscotch, Horseshoes, Jump Rope, and Basketball were
played outdoors. Wolf Over the River was an outside game. A

line of players joined hands and called, "Red Rover, Red Rover, let Billy come over." And Billy would run toward the line and try to break through. Players had to hold on tight to prevent someone from breaking the chain.

Indoor games included Jacks and Moon, played with dominoes.

Spin the Bottle was played indoors. A person in the middle of a circle spun a bottle. Whoever it pointed to got to go walking with the person who spun the bottle.

Paper dolls were popular for girls to play with.

All types of tag games were popular. They had "base" games. The base was a safe place for players. They couldn't be tagged or found if they were in the base area. It was a sort of king's X land.

Annie over the House was a ball game played by two teams on either side of the house. One team yelled "Annie," and the other team with the ball said, "Over," and threw the ball over the house. If the receiving team caught the ball, team members ran to the other side of the house and tried to tag people on the other side. Each person tagged went on their team. The team with the most members won.

Popping the Whip: All join hands, then form a line with the big kids at one end. They start running as fast as they can, and the ones in front turn sharply and bring the little ones around, almost breaking their necks.

Tops: Some of the finest top spinners in the country came from East Texas. The tops had spikes sharp enough to bust another top while it was spinning. Contests were held to see who could bust up the most tops.

Go in and out the Window: Everyone holds hands and forms a big circle, with one person in the middle. They go round and round and sing, "Go in and out the window, for we have gained this day," three times, then hold their hands up, and the person in the middle goes in and out between the people and sings the song three times. When she has finished, she goes back in the middle and the people start singing, "Go forth and face your lover, for we have gained this day," three times. The person she picks gets down on his knees and says, "I kneel because I love you, for we have gained this day."

Then they get up, and the person they have picked stays in the middle. The other one goes out and they play it over and over. If a boy is in the middle, he picks a girl. If a girl is in the middle, she picks a boy.

School closings: At the end of school every year, all the parents and youngsters would gather at the school for a meal and a program by the school kids. This was a big social event of the year, and kids would show their best talents on stage.

Corn Huskin's: Early in the day, you'd get the corn into the back porch or lawn and start shuckin'. Prizes were given to the ones who found the red ear, the first speckled ear, and the biggest ear. The one who picked the most corn also won a prize. It took most of the day and part of the night to husk all the corn. Sometimes a dance would end the evening.

Square dances were popular, drawing large numbers of people from a wide area. Usually one man would fiddle and another did the calling.

Round dancing parties were popular, too. Music was from a harmonica, violin, and accordion. The furniture was moved out of the biggest room in the house, and stumps were placed around the room. Then planks were brought in for the youngsters to sit on. Most everyone rode horseback or walked to the parties, which lasted at least four hours. On Saturday nights they ended by eleven o'clock so everyone would have time to get a good night's rest before going to church.

Rodeos: When cattle were being dipped for fever ticks, boys would herd the steers and heifers and ride them on weekends. They rode horses or mules bareback. Sometimes somebody would get a carload and go to rodeos. Prize money was small, but people went mostly to watch.

Horse traders would come to town in wagons with a whole string of ponies behind them. They stopped in town to swap horses.

Tacky Parties: Small prizes such as combs were given to the person dressed the tackiest. Men would wear one overall suspender hanging down; women might wear men's shoes. These were the forerunners of today's costume parties. Sometimes people tried to disguise themselves.

Washers: A game played at minimum cost and maximum

enjoyment. Probably grew from the game of "dollars," where players pitched silver dollars at two holes in the ground twenty-one feet apart. Whoever got closest to the hole or had the best score won the game.

If two people played, each contestant stood together at one hole and pitched toward the other hole. They then would talk to the other hole and pitch back. Each contestant had four washers or dollars. If four people played, partners were chosen and one of each team stood at each hole.

"Leaners" were washers just far enough over the hole to see through the hole of the washer into the hole in the ground. Leaners were worth three points.

A sunk washer brought five points.

"Outer-closet" described washers which are neither sinkers nor leaners and were worth only one point.

Washers also canceled each other out. If one team made five points and the next team also made five, the second team's five canceled out the first team's five.

The winner pitched first in the next round.

A score of twenty-one constituted a game, and in the case of a tie, you followed the rule of sudden death, or whoever scores first wins.

Washer pitching requires a high degree of concentration.

Box suppers were popular pioneer functions. The boxes of food were auctioned off to the highest male bidder, who got to eat with the female who prepared the meal. The boxes contained such items as fried chicken, potato salad, pickles, deviled eggs, and chocolate pie.

The boxes were decorated with ruffles and bows. If it was election year, the candidates would be on hand, and they would buy several suppers. Music and entertainment would be provided. It would thrill a girl when her box brought a big price. Sometimes a girl would slip around and tell a boy what her box looked like so he could outbid the others. Some prices were $5. On some occasions, a box would bring $15.

Some creators of box suppers were very inventive. Some made them in the forms of houses, stoves, dressers, mailboxes, and flags. One woman made a box in the shape of an airplane with wheels on it.

Money from box suppers went to buy things for the school or church or community center. Parents always went to parties with their kids and had as much fun as the youngsters, who enjoyed seeing the adults enjoying themselves.

Ice cream suppers, Sunday singings, watermelon cuts, and apple bitings provided plenty of fun. In the latter, an apple would be hung on a string and a couple would try to eat it from opposite sides.

There was always a blending of work and social functions. When women had sewing to do, they did it at the sewing circle. Sometimes they worked on individual items; other times they worked together on one item, such as a quilt. It was a big event to get together with your neighbors and work with them to produce something special like a quilt.

Pounding parties were given when a new person moved into the area. These were for the new preacher, newlyweds, or someone who was leaving. Everyone brought an item of food, or sometimes other things. They'd serve refreshments. The custom continues in some parts of East Texas today.

Barn raisings were community events, too. If someone got burned out or had some other type of misfortune, all the neighbors would pitch in and help rebuild, sometimes even supplying the materials. The women always served food, and kids played games.

The Old Parlor Organ

Vernon Schuder lives at Riverside, a small community near Huntsville. She has an old pump organ in her living room. She loves to play "Amazing Grace" on it. "It sounds so much prettier than when it's played on the piano," comments Vernon. "And the organ has a different touch. On the organ, you don't take your fingers off the keys and bounce as you do on a piano. You slide from one key to another to keep the music going all the time.

"I started playing organ in church sixty-one years ago. I was eleven years old and was forced into it because the two young ladies in the community who had played the organ in church both got married and moved away. It was little Vernon or none."

The first song she played in church was "I Am Resolved." "It has a bass run in it, and I was stupid enough to try to play it when I got to it. Cousin Jesse Atkinson was standing right by the organ singing. I should have let him just roar out that bass run all by himself. But I tried it. I didn't have enough fingers. I balled it up good and was so embarrassed. I was just trompin' those pedals with the ends of my toes because I was so small."

She went up to the church house during the week and learned how to play "I Am Resolved." "I was resolved to learn that song," says Vernon. "I learned how to double my thumb under so I'd have enough fingers to play that song."

Vernon remembers as a child watching those other two young ladies who played the organ in church. There was no air conditioning. The services would be long, and if you were pumping with both feet, singing with your mouth, and playing with both hands, you got pretty hot.

"These two young ladies would have their boyfriends (we called them beaus then) to stand by them and fan them with a cardboard fan as they played. I thought how romantic that would be. But being eleven years old, I had to get along for a while with a girl cousin standing by me and fanning me. But by the time I was fourteen, I had a beau to stand by me and fan me. And I married that one."

Her husband often made the remark that if he ever got the chance, he would buy her an old pump organ. Churches were doing away with them then, switching to pianos.

They had been married a number of years when a traveling evangelist and his wife came through Oakhurst, just down the road. The love offering wasn't enough to get them down the road to the next town. And the evangelist's wife let it be known that she would sell her organ for fifty dollars cash.

"I don't guess there was a soul in Oakhurst that had fifty dollars," says Vernon, "but she heard that my husband was looking for an organ like that, so she went to the only telephone in Oakhurst and phoned over here to the only phone in town (down at the drugstore), and my husband took two grown men and a pickup to Oakhurst to buy that organ."

The lady wanted to know if the organ would be treated right. She said, "I don't want it played in no honky-tonk."

Vernon's husband told the lady the story of how when he courted Vernon he would stand by the organ and fan her while she played for church services. He told the lady he wanted it for sentimental reasons. She sold it to Vernon's husband, and he hauled it home. It occupies a prominent spot in the main room of Vernon's house.

"It still plays. I play it all the time and think about the days when I used to play an organ like that for church."

I asked Vernon to play "I Am Resolved" on the organ. She did and sang along as she played. When she got to the line that says "I will hasten to Him, hasten so glad and free" and the bass comes in with "hasten so glad and free," she got it just right. I was watching her thumb. She doubled it under.

A Real Sting

Old Man Ashworth is all crippled up with arthritis and spends most of his time out in an open shed under a fan. An electronic bug zapper hangs from the edge of the shed roof.

His only income is from his Social Security check. He makes wine from wild grapes. Mr. Ashworth saves his money in coffee cans, which he hides throughout his house.

Last week he called Fred, his good friend, and asked him to come over. Ash needed some help. When Fred arrived, he found the floor of Ash's home covered in coins of all denominations. An empty coffee can was on the desk by the phone.

Fred asked, "What happened here, Ash?"

Ash replied, "Come on and I'll show you."

They went into the bedroom, where Ash showed Fred three different coffee cans in a dresser drawer, by his night-stand, and under his pillow.

"Don't ever open them cans, Fred," cautioned Ash. "They've all got copperheads in them. I keep them on top of my change to guard it."

All the coffee cans had plastic sealers on top with slits in

them so the snakes could get some air. Ash went on to divulge the names of his pet guard snakes.

Fred asked, "Did you have a copperhead in that can in the living room?"

Ash replied that he did.

"And where is it?" asked Fred.

"That's Oscar. I caught him a little bit ago and put him in another coffee can."

"Do you know who tried to get your money?"

"'Course I do," says Ash. "That kid down the road came here wanting to use the phone. I was out under the shed. That boy came out rubbing his hand and running like crazy for home. When I came in, change was all over everywhere and Oscar was coiled up in a corner over there."

The phone rang. It was the boy's mother. "Mr. Ashworth," she said, "you'd better do something about those wasps at your house. I just got back from the doctor. He said he had never seen such a violent reaction to a wasp sting as my boy had."

Ash promised to be careful and watch the wasps, then went out to his favorite place near the bug zapper and sat down to contemplate things.

Laughter in the Woods

Bob Murphey of Nacogdoches is a lawyer, banker, rancher, and notary public. He's also a humorist. "People are hungry for good clean humor," he says. He specializes in rural or backwoods humor. "It doesn't matter how big the city is or whether someone was born under neon lights, people understand it and like it."

Bob has practiced law in East Texas for forty years. He has been a county attorney and a district attorney and has served in the legislature, but mostly he is known as the guy who makes humorous speeches.

When I visited with him, it was raining. "This rain we've been having reminds me of an old boy in south Nacogdoches County who was worried about his cattle after a heavy rain. He went down to the bottom behind his place that had a creek running through it. That creek had done got so high you could see under it.

"He had a pickup settin' by the side of the house. It rained so hard it filled the bed of his pickup level with water. And the tailgate was down on it, too."

He gets his stories from kinfolks, friends, and neighbors. "Most of 'em I pick up around the courthouses, the benches where the old-timers sit and spit and whittle. Most of them were told to me as true incidents that either happened to Uncle Clem or Aunt Jessie Mae or somebody. All of them just as humorous as they could be."

He calls a levelheaded East Texan "one where the snuff runs out of both sides of his mouth." He calls overalls an East Texas tuxedo. He refers to buzzards as the East Texas sanitation department.

"Then I tell about the little boy who was eatin' breakfast one morning. He was soppin' syrup with good ol' homemade biscuits. He had already chopped up his butter and stirred it in the syrup, and he was draggin' that biscuit through there and finally got it all soaked up. After eatin' that tasty mouthful, he decided to fix another batch. He poured the syrup in the plate, took the knife to get some more butter, and his momma reached over and backhanded him. Knocked him plumb outa that cane-bottom chair onto the linoleum. She shook her finger at him and said, 'Junior, if I've told you once I've told you a thousand times, lick your knife before you stick it in that butter.'"

Murphey has been master of ceremonies for Lufkin's Hushpuppy Olympics several times. One year when a visiting congressman from Michigan won the political category, Bob told a story. He said he had a friend who went to work in a defense plant in Detroit during World War II. Finally V-E Day came, and when he reported to work the next morning he told his fellow workers, "Boys, I'm going back home to East Texas. Where y'all goin'?" One of them replied, "We aren't going any-

where. We live here." The Texan turned to him and said, "You mean there's people livin' up here when there ain't no war goin' on?"

If Bob Murphey is awake, chances are he's chewing tobacco. He makes it an art. "Lots of people wonder why I don't spit much. After you chew awhile, you just kinda let it lay there so you can enjoy the flavor. Women and children spit a lot, but professional chewers don't have to spit much."

He thinks tobacco-spitting contests are for amateurs. "I never did put much importance on how far a person could spit. But accuracy is another thing. My wife calls that to my attention frequently around the house. She tells me I ain't as accurate as I used to be."

He tells the story of two older women at a concert in the park. They were a little late, and music was playing when they arrived. One of them said, "You know, I believe that's a waltz from Strauss." The other one said she didn't know, but there was a sign near the bandstand, so she went to read it. In a moment she came back and said, "No, it's a refrain from spittin'."

The Fire Ant Festival in Marshall

A lot of cities in Texas stage festivals in October, featuring beer, sausage, and oompah bands. But not Marshall. That city has an October spectacular that revolves around the fire ant.

The annual Marshall Fire Ant Festival takes place the second weekend of October. Among other things, it has the largest parade in East Texas. Some of the more than 120 entries are weird, such as the Shriner Training Academy. Unlike the zany fez-wearing Shriners who drive small cars in parades, the training academy folks perform their intricate maneuvers in bottomless cardboard boxes shaped like cars. They run around and say things like "I can't wait until I become a Shriner." Weird.

Past winners of the parade include the Committee for the Right to Arm Bears, which featured a man in a bear suit carrying a shotgun, and the Synchronized Dry Land Swim Team, which did an out-of-the-water routine to "Walking to New Orleans."

The Fire Ant Festival features some of the most creative contests in the state. Like the Fire Ant calling contest. Judges and contestants start out even, because nobody knows what one sounds like.

Contestants have to make three distinct calls: an alarm call, a mating call, and a feeding call. The only rule is you have to keep it clean.

One winner did a "Fire Ant Rap." One eighty-year-old contestant whistled through a gas hose.

There's also the World Championship Fire Ant Roundup. They round up fire ants just like West Texans round up rattlesnakes. The winner gets a big trophy and $150.

George Smith, one of the coordinators of the event, says gathering fire ants is not easy. "One lady called and asked if she could use a vacuum cleaner. We told her she could, but she had to get them out of the bag into an official jug. She said she'd have to work on that."

One contestant uses a tub of water to round up fire ants. He digs up an ant bed and throws it in the tub of water. The dirt sinks, the ants float, and he skims them off and puts them in the jug.

Determining the amount of ants brought in presents a problem. "You can't count them," says George. "We weigh the jugs, then weigh them again with the ants in them. We use electronic postal scales. Last year's winner brought in thirty-eight hundredths of an ounce. That's probably about 15,000 ants, give or take a couple of thousand."

The Rubber Chicken Chunking Contest is part of the fun, too. It's like punt, pass, and kick, only contestants use a rubber chicken. They throw it for accuracy and distance. The current world's record is 192 feet.

The World Championship Beverage Coaster Throw gets

lots of entries. The record there is seventy-eight feet. Other events include washer and horseshoe pitching, the Fire Ant Costume Contest, the Fire Ant Diaper Derby (baby races), and the Poker Chip in the Haystack Contest.

All kinds of entertainment, from local magicians to well known musicians, takes place throughout the weekend.

The event attracts 50,000 people, which is double the population of Marshall.

Past festivals featured the Texas Open Ugly Face Contest, a Tour de Fire Ant Bike Race, a Fire Ant 5-K Chase, arts and crafts, and a chili cook-off in which every cook has to put at least one fire ant in the pot.

A street dance is named the Fire Ant Stomp. Fire Ant mascots Freedy, Elvira, and Baby Sugar welcome guests. Marshall residents say they wanted to turn a negative into a positive. They've done that with the Fire Ant Festival.

Words of Wisdom

Bill Brett used to be postmaster of Hull. He has written a few books on life in the East Texas woods. Being a writer, he knows the value of words. He also knows that when a certain phrase pops into his mind, he needs to write it down, or it'll be gone.

That's why Bill keeps a little notebook in his shirt pocket. He writes in it a lot. He'll hear something worth remembering and he'll make a note of it in his notebook.

He has been carrying little notebooks for years and has filled several of them. He keeps them in stacks at his home in the woods.

The last time we were together, he got out his little notebook and we went over some of the things written in it.

On people who like natural food: "Do you think it bothers these natural-food people that when they die there might be preservatives added?"

He keeps quotes from famous people like Al Capone: "You

can get much further with a kind word and a gun than with just a kind word."

On politics: "A fool and his money is soon elected."

On equality: "Women who seek to be equal to men don't have much ambition."

Bill pulled out a quote by Edgar Allan Poe: "I have great faith in fools. Self confidence, my friends call it."

"A friend of mine said he had eaten so many rabbits every time a dog barked he'd run toward the briar patch."

On committees: "The eleventh commandment is: Thou shalt not committee."

"These two fellows were talking one time and one of them said, 'I done something last week I ain't never done before.' The other one said, 'What was it?' The first one replied, 'I quit

smoking and drinking, and went on a diet. It was the longest three hours I ever spent in my life.'"

Bill has a Mark Twain quote: "That feller ain't got no more principles than a congressman."

On raising a good garden: "Don't never plant more than your wife can work."

Bill Brett has some favorite quotes like this one, which makes so many sportsmen mad: "They ain't nothin' as healthy and uplifting as bein' out in the fresh air and sunshine slaughterin' God's little creatures."

On low cattle prices: "Last week I stole two cows and lost eighty dollars on them."

He has an old Estonian proverb: "He who flatters the mother will hug the daughter."

Around Hull they have changed that somewhat: "We call it licking the cow to catch the calf."

A bachelor around Hull took up with a widow woman who had a young son, and the bachelor was spending lots of time with the boy. Bill said he was following common horse sense: "When you break a colt to lead, the mare usually follows."

On school boards: "The lord made idiots for practice, then made school boards."

Bill says it's amazing how these things pile up. "I've got hundreds of them. I just write 'em down when I run across them, then later when I'm looking at them I'm surprised that I was carrying so much wisdom around in my pocket."

Another East Texan with a keen insight is Gurley Sanders of Athens, who wrote a newspaper column for years in the *Athens Review*. He put his writings into a book, and called it *Gurleyver's Travels*.

The introduction states, "A life after death was never envisioned for these essays. It was the stranger passing through who resurrected them." It seems a lady from Pennsylvania came to Athens, stayed a year, and upon leaving to go back north suggested the columns be issued in book form.

Some of Gurley's pronouncements:

"Fifty to sixty wars are now in progress on earth, which is about average for civilized planets."

"Disease germs work at their trade with the single-minded zeal of a federal judge wrecking a school system."

"A man prays more fervently when being chased by a bear than he does while sitting smugly in a Cadillac."

"Old age has its compensations, chief of which is freedom from the obligation to succeed."

"Planet Earth is a mental institution for the universe."

"Redheaded people are a minority group in the United States, legitimately entitled to certain dispensations and preferential treatment from the government."

Corbett Akins at Large

"I was born in Panola County on a Friday morning at five o'clock. Eighteen hundred and ninety two. I took the name of Clifford. I kept it for six months. When I was six months old, Jim Corbett and John L. Sullivan had a fight and I was bouncin' so on the bed my papa came in from the field and named me Jim Corbett. He said a boy that rough and tough ought to be a prize fighter."

Corbett Akins worked with his father on the family farm until he was twenty-one years old, the age his father said he could leave.

"My last day on the farm I broke land all day with a one mule-turnin' plow. I came in that night and I was so tired I could hardly move. I told my daddy I was leavin' home the next morning, which would be my twenty-first birthday. He asked me to stay and told me he needed me on the farm. I told him I'd never plow another furrow as long as I live."

The next morning, Corbett and his dad hooked up a team and drove to Beckville. They went to the People's State Bank and borrowed thirty-three dollars. The interest was three dollars. Corbett's dad handed over three ten-dollar bills to Corbett and told him goodbye.

"I went down to the railroad. And I can hear that whistle

today. She sounds lonesome. I didn't hardly know what a train was. But after awhile a long, slow freight came by. I grabbed the bars on the side of the boxcar and climbed on. I rode it to Longview. I got on another train to Fort Worth and then just rambled all over the United States."

At Wichita, Kansas, he came across a Salvation Army band with tambourines and drums and harps. One tall woman threw her head back and sang, "O where is my boy tonight? Once as pure as the morning dew, O where is my boy tonight?"

" 'Course, that threw my feet under the dinner table at home. I knew I oughta be home," says Corbett. But he didn't go home. He went on to a small town in Oklahoma. He had twenty-five cents to his name. He went to a carnival and saw a man pitching baseballs at a keg.

"You got three balls for a dime. And every time you put a ball in the keg, you got a dollar. I watched people throw for some time, then I started throwing. In just a little while I had six dollars. And the man running the outfit wouldn't let me pitch anymore. A man with a badge and a pistol walked up and asked me what was the matter. I told him. The lawman told the man I could pitch or he would have to close. The man closed his concession. I decided right then I wanted to be a sheriff."

Near Hutchinson, Kansas, Corbett walked into a little store and encountered the store owner. "He looked like Santa Claus. His beard came down to his navel. I told him I was hungry, that I hadn't had anything to eat in three or four days. That man went back to the cheese rack, cut me off a big chunk, and put it in a sack. He reached into the cracker barrel and filled the sack with crackers and handed it to me. He told me to get an onion, which I did. I went out back where there was a windmill and ate everything."

After roaming the country for a while, Corbett decided to return home. He caught a train which was filled with rutabaga turnips. He ate dozens of them. Very early one Sunday morning, he and a fellow traveler landed in Fort Worth. They saw a milkman putting bottles of milk on the front steps of homes in the area. One of the bottles had the phrase "pure cream" written on it. Corbett's traveling companion picked it up, drank about half of it, and gave the rest to Corbett. "That cream, with the turnips we had, made a good meal."

Corbett went on to Terrell, worked for a while, then bought a train ticket back home to Beckville. He was later elected Sheriff of Panola County and held the post for many years.

Fall Foliage in East Texas

From mid-October through November, autumn is awesome in East Texas. The trails through the woods lead to color, harvest festivals, fun, and excitement. After the first arctic frost sparks the season's gala transformation, deer and squirrels start to move around and geese take to flight.

If you've chuckled over the thought of Texans getting out and driving around East Texas looking at the fall colors, you just don't know about our forests. Some autumn hues in East Texas are as dazzling as those in New England.

Our woods peak later than those in the northeast. The East Texas color change occurs from late October until Thanksgiving, usually reaching its peak around the second week in November.

East Texas forests have five distinct varieties of maple trees, fourteen species of oaks, six species of hickory, plus sweet gums, dogwoods, sumac, sassafras, birch, and walnut. The colors range from yellows to golds to reds to deep purples.

Four large national forests are located

in East Texas in addition to the Big Thicket National Preserve. Parks and freshwater lakes are numerous in East Texas.

The East Texas Tourism Association has a toll-free number to call for the latest information on fall foliage (1-800-262-8747). Forty foliage spotters in a forty-five-county hardwood/pine forest area volunteer their help each year.

During autumn months, in an area that stretches from Texarkana to Woodville, elms and hackberries sport cloaks of

gold deepening almost to orange. Black gums and sumac are blushing in crimson, and sweet gums are turning gold to red.

Pumpkins, gourds, and cans of syrup tastefully displayed at roadside stands; colorful quilts seen hanging on clotheslines; leaves, pine cones, sweet gum balls, grapevine wreaths, and spicy bouquets of flowers and tawny grasses make great souvenirs to remember your trip through the East Texas woods in the fall.

Black Gold

Long before the legendary oil booms at Spindletop and Kilgore, a little place called Oil Springs, not far from Nacogdoches, was producing oil. It is the site of the first oil boom in Texas. Indians used the slimy substance seeping from the ground to rub on their bodies to ward off evil spirits, thinking it was some type of potion the gods had sent down to them. Later residents used the oil to soften leather and to grease axles.

The oily springs fascinated Tol Barret, a merchant who became the first wildcatter in Texas. He nearly brought in the first oil producer in the nation. But that distinction goes to Drake, Pennsylvania. In 1859, a short while after the Drake discovery, Barret acquired a lease around the oily springs. But the Civil War and a lack of proper equipment prevented him from drilling for oil.

Seven years later, he drilled 106 feet into the ground with a steam-powered auger and brought in a ten-barrel-a-day producer. Believing great wealth was just ahead, he capped the well and headed out by stagecoach to Pennsylvania to seek capital and machinery. He wrote his wife from Shreveport on November 1, 1866: "The prospects of making a large amount of money are as flattering as they can be."

Barret returned home with $5,000 worth of machinery and sank a new hole near Oil Springs, but it yielded no oil. Barret, disgusted and bankrupt, returned to his store.

A small company of investors brought in a 250-barrel well near the springs in 1877 and started the first oil boom in Texas.

Fortune hunters flocked to the area and built a skimming plant, a barrel factory, and an inadequate pipeline. In winter the line clogged, and workers had to build pine-knot fires under it to keep the oil flowing.

A visitor to the boomtown wrote: "The whole place was alive with tents, houses, oil derricks, and men, women and children. Charlie Byrd ran a hack to Nacogdoches and back every day, bringing passengers to Oil City. Oil excitement ran high. The oil company had a large boarding house. Their men made barrels and tubs at the factory. Hammers and saws were heard in every direction."

But the boom didn't last. Drillers soon exhausted the shallow pool beneath the forest floor and wandered away to other oil fields, surrendering the town to underbrush.

Other efforts were made to drill in the field after the turn of the century, but with no success. Today, the fountainhead of the Texas oil industry has little to show for its past. Just a few old storage tanks, some unused casings that jut out from the earth, and a spring of oily, bitter water.

East Texans in older days were poor. When they saw a chance to earn some money, they took it. So with the promise of wealth coming on at increasing regularity, even the poorest East Texan felt his day was just around the corner.

And for some, it was.

Dad Joiner

Columbus Marvin (Dad) Joiner brought in a successful test on the No. 3 Daisy Bradford oil well on the Juan Ximenes survey about seven miles from Henderson on the evening of September 5, 1930, thus opening up the largest oil field in the world up to that time (the largest until later discoveries in the Middle East). Dad had been in the area three years with a

shoestring operation. Miss Daisy Bradford had staked Joiner his last $100 needed to bring in the discovery well.

A crowd of two thousand people looked on as oil gushed over the top of the derrick from 3,580 feet below the earth. By midnight, Henderson was full of people making deals for leases and royalties. Bottles of crude oil were brought into town to convince the skeptical.

The Daisy Bradford had changed the mood of the entire area from an agriculture-oriented community to that of a

bustling oil town. Nearly all the land around the well was owned by individuals. Large oil companies became eager buyers, and farmers were reluctant to sell immediately, holding out for more money until the well proved itself. Finally, on that famous October 3, the gusher was brought under control and the oil was routed into storage tanks.

By October 4, fifteen thousand people crowded into Henderson. The oil companies paid landowners in cash. The East Texas Oil Field, as it became known, covered the counties of Upshur, Gregg, Rusk, Smith, and Cherokee. By July of 1931, a total of 1,100 wells had been drilled. By the end of the year, the total was 3,396. During one week in October, one well was completed every hour. Peak production from the field was 205,000,000 barrels in 1933.

C. M. Joiner was born near Center Star, Alabama, in 1860. He began a law practice in Tennessee in 1883 and was a member of the legislature of that state from 1889 to 1891. He moved in 1897 to Oklahoma, where he made and lost two fortunes in oil before coming to Texas in 1926.

In the autumn of 1930, Columbus Marion Joiner was looking for oil on Daisy Bradford's farm in Rusk County. He had come to East Texas with $45 dollars in his pocket. He quoted the Bible to the men and poetry to the women. He began buying up oil leases from farmers. Some of the leases were bought with cash, but most with scrip, and most were for $1 an acre.

Geologists had already explored the land. To them, East Texas was barren, worthless. Most thought any oil around might be deep and not favorable for commercial development.

The geologists left, the wildcatters left after drilling seventeen dry holes, and the major oil companies walked away.

Dad Joiner brought in A. D. Lloyd, who was a chemist with a colorful and checkered past. Lloyd was seventy-three, weighed 320 pounds, and called himself "Doc." He had been a druggist, veterinarian, and government chemist and drifted west during the Idaho gold rush. He had prospected for gold and oil in the Yukon and Mexico. He had been married six times and had peddled patent medicines made from oil.

In 1927 Lloyd told Joiner that he felt oil would be found in the woodbine sand at 3,550 feet. He drew straight lines to connect every major oil field in the country. His prediction was that oil would be found where all of those lines intersected. They intersected in East Texas.

Joiner convinced Daisy Bradford to lease him 925.5 acres for 50¢ an acre. Joiner sold leases for two years to raise money to drill.

He started putting pipe into the ground. At 2,000 feet the pipe stuck. He tried a second time and the drill pipe twisted off at 2,518 feet. The third try was sunk where the skid moving the rig cracked when it caught on a rock. By late March in 1930, the well had reached 2,600 feet.

On October 5, the earth trembled and oil gushed over the top of the rig. It hit at 3,580 feet, thirty feet deeper than Lloyd had predicted. Lloyd was remarkably accurate when describing the shape of the East Texas field. It was thirty-five miles long, five miles wide, and covered 85,000 acres of production.

Joiner owed more to his creditors than he was making. Some of the leases had been sold several times, and everyone wanted to be paid. He went into receivership and spent most of his time in court. He began negotiating with H. L. Hunt to purchase a majority interest in 4,400 acres of the Rusk County oil leases.

H. L. Hunt bought Joiner's leases for $30,000 cash, four short-term notes totaling $45,000 and $1.26 million to be paid out of production from the lease. Within days, Joiner was offered more than $3 million for his holdings. It was too late. The deal had already been made in Dallas.

Hunt soon discovered that he had a good title to only two and a half acres. He began clearing the titles, buying royalty from each landowner. He settled more than 250 lawsuits. He won them all, settling most out of court for $250 or less.

Shortly after his transaction with Joiner, Hunt began drilling a well of his own and building a pipeline. He was turned down for a loan from the Overton bank. A Mrs. Tucker, who ran the boarding house where Dad Joiner lived, loaned $5,000 to Hunt. When he returned a few weeks later to pay her, she said, "Just send me the interest each month. I'll let you know when I want the principal." It was a good investment.

For his famous discovery well, Joiner used a flimsy pine rig and battered tools. Miss Daisy Bradford had staked Dad Joiner the last $100 to bring in the discovery well. Broke and in debt but hopeful, his third drilling effort was successful. He became known as "the Father of the East Texas Oil Field" and acquired the nickname "Dad." He retired in Dallas in 1940 and died there in 1947. The town of Joinerville was named for him. The town, previously called Cyril, was once a cluster of modest homes located about six miles west of Henderson on the Tyler highway. As traffic increased, the town grew. Joinerville once had a population of 10,000 and a school with 800 students, the largest rural school in the world.

The land around Joinerville had been worn out from too many years of cotton farming. You couldn't make much money in 1929 and 1930. The only money was provided by the lady of the house who sold butter and eggs on Saturdays.

Texans look forward to conquering new worlds instead of wallowing in the self-pity of lost battles. The East Texas Oil Field created excitement and the anticipation of great wealth.

It was the California gold rush, the Klondike, the Oklahoma land rush, and the wildest of past oil booms all rolled into one. The daring, the resourceful, and the unscrupulous had caught the scent of oil and money, and they swooped down on the five counties like flies to a dead cow.

People who settled East Texas brought with them the ideas and aspirations of the antebellum cotton economy, the plantation system based on slave labor. When the Civil War broke out, young men went off to fight for the South, their homeland. After the war, the plantations slowly disappeared, replaced with a system of tenant farming and sharecropping, keeping the former slaves and impoverished white people bound to the land with little hope beyond survival.

It's hard to remain soft-spoken, polite, and hospitable when your fierce pride is hurt because no money is coming in. Life was hard, but not cheerless. The food was good. Mealtimes were special, and people looked forward to better times. It was the only life people knew anything about. Religion was a powerful force. The community church was the center of activity.

The discovery of oil brought a transfusion of money, and the lives of the people would never be the same. It was like a third-world country suddenly invaded by a civilization with sophisticated technology.

Dallas jewelry store owners opened their stores on Sunday mornings and after-hours to accommodate the newly rich East Texans. Jack Elder of Kilgore tells about his dad, Frank Elder, buying a Tavannes watch with a platinum chain for 5,000 barrels of oil, which was selling for 10¢ a barrel. The transaction was made on a Sunday morning at Linz Jewelers in Dallas. Mr. Linz lived in the Adolphus Hotel then. Jack acquired the watch from his dad, then passed it on to his son. The signatures of the three owners are engraved on the back of the watch. Jack says the engraver was appalled at the request to put the names on the watch. "He knew he would have to put three different signatures on the back of a fine watch. But after a sufficient amount of money changed hands, the engraver took a few healthy belts of whiskey and did the beautiful work."

In his book titled *Gaston High School, Joinerville, Texas,* William Jack tells some wonderful stories about the impact of sudden wealth on unsophisticated people. One elderly lady, who lived near Turnertown, had secretly yearned for only two things in life: a black wig and a monkey. When the first lease money came in, she promptly bought both and sashayed among her envious neighbors, even in church, with the wig in place and the monkey on her shoulder.

Oil is not fair. While some Tyler families built mansions with gold-plated bathroom fixtures, others struggled along with a privy and a chamber pot. Some residents didn't like the idea of having bathrooms in the house, and some men threw fits when gas lines were extended into their homes. A number-three tub, an outhouse, and a fireplace were all a man needed. And who needed to travel to faraway places? One man took a ride to Tyler in a wagon, and that satisfied all his travel yearnings.

East Texans feel a sweet melancholy about the place where they live, brought on partly by the people and events that have shaped their lives. A well, a tree, a storm cellar, and a spring all represent distinctive memories.

The distance in space between Tyler and a small town is just a few miles. The distance in time is three or four decades.

The Glory Days

Drought is a constant threat to farmers and ranchers. Just after the Wall Street crash, East Texans found themselves slaves to the sun and the cycles of nature no man can control. The only thing was hope. Hope for rain, hope for gentle winds, hope for a crop.

The farmer planted his seeds and prayed to his God and sang the blues while his family ate peas almost every time the table was set. Purple-hull peas. Cream peas. Crowder peas. Black-eyed peas. Always peas.

One farmer hitched up his bib overalls, kicked the sand from his brogans, and swore that he ran out to the pea patch and lay face down when he saw a cyclone come swarming across those rolling hills.

"Why?" his neighbor asked.

"Well," the farmer drawled, "that pea patch has saved my life a lot of times, and I had no reason to believe it would let me down this time."

He, like so many others, was convinced that the blood running through his veins was, by now, at least ninety percent pea soup.

In the midst of the oil boom in East Texas, Kilgore appointed a Chief of Police who had no use for armed bandits. He stopped two men on the street one day and angrily told them, "You fellows just got out of the pen. If you had stayed in the pen for forty years, you would have been looking for somebody to hijack just as soon as you got out. You're looking for somebody now. But I'm in this town and you fellows can't stay. Get out, and get out now." His words were law.

The next afternoon, the two men held up a grocery store, took the money from the safe, and fled with lawmen close behind. The chief, on his way home, saw them driving too fast and too reckless as they crossed the railroad tracks. He braked his auto, reached for his rifle, and fired. The first shot got the driver's neck. The getaway car spun out of control. As the other man leaped for safety, a second shot cut him down.

An officer yelled at the chief, "How did you know those two had robbed a store? We thought you were in Longview."

"I didn't know," the chief barked. "It's just that I told them to get out of town yesterday, and they didn't go."

Texas Ranger Lone Wolf Gonzaullas spent two weeks in Kilgore dressed like a bum, hanging out in the roughest establishments. When he had a feel for the town and its characters, he cleaned up, put on his Texas Ranger badge, and rode into town on a black stallion. He, too, had his own brand of justice. When he saw a stranger in the street, he stopped the man and asked what he was doing. If the man replied he was looking for a job, Gonzaullas asked what kind of work he did. If he said he was a roughneck, Gonzaullas would slowly and meticulously examine the palms of their hands. If they were callused, rough, and stained with grease and dirt, the ranger merely nodded and moved on. But if they were smooth and clean, he jailed the stranger without another word. Gonzaullas felt those kind of hands belonged to con men and thieves too lazy to work.

One night, Lone Wolf Gonzaullas, partner Bob Goss, and every lawman he could trust raided every honky-tonk, beer joint, pool hall, dance hall, domino parlor, gambling den, and dive. There was no jail big enough to hold all 300 prisoners, so they were herded to a wooded corner and hooked up to a homemade trotline made out of log chains that had been stretched around the trees. Later, pews were ripped out of an abandoned Baptist church, and the trotline was dragged into the sweltering interior of the little wooden building. The prisoners were fed once a day. A tin can was passed down the line and used for a urinal. They were held by padlocked collars which rubbed their necks raw. Gonzaullas and Goss offered to let them off the chain if they could get out of town in four hours. No one refused. Few were ever baptized in the trotline Baptist church more than once. The two rangers controlled the town, and crimes of violence began to ebb.

Lone Wolf Gonzaullas would not lie down for a shave. He sat erect, facing the door, his hands never far from twin pearl-handled revolvers. He wanted to be in a position to see who walked in before they saw him. A Texas Ranger didn't have a lot of friends, not when he kept peace in a city that had no peace.

When Dad Joiner struck pay dirt, oil was selling for $1.10 a barrel. Before 1931 had ended, the price skidded to 6¢, sometimes 2¢ a barrel. A well that cost $12,000 to drill had to produce 200,000 barrels just to break even.

May 1, 1931, the Texas Railroad Commission issued an order limiting the field to 160,000 barrels a day. The oilmen filed a barrage of court injunctions against the edict and defiantly kept pumping.

Martial law was declared by Governor Ross Sterling, and all wells were shut down on August 17. Nothing had been said about drilling, so the oilmen kept drilling, and no one was able to stop them.

The Methodist, Baptist, and Presbyterian churches in

Kilgore all exploded and burned on August 22. For a time, Kilgore was known as the town without a church. A seed house, gin, wholesale grocery, rooming house, morgue, and grain warehouse were also set on fire. For twenty-one days, national guardsmen kept the lid clamped on the town. Observation planes patrolled by air, and cavalry rode with Texas Rangers through the oil belt to make sure the shutdown of "the greatest stream of crude in the world" was complete.

The field was finally brought to a semblance of order in the fall of 1933. Within three months, the price of oil had risen to 83¢. But bootleg oil from little tea-kettle refineries shipped out of East Texas caused it to slip at an alarming rate. More than 100 million barrels of illegal oil were smuggled from the field.

President Franklin D. Roosevelt had to ban the illegal oil from interstate commerce before the situation was able to be controlled.

From 1930 until 1944, the East Texas field produced an estimated 2 billion barrels of oil, twice as much as any other field in the U.S. The oil was said to be the best the world ever knew. Kilgore became a famous place for photographers to take pictures of downtown drilling rigs crowded together on the richest city block in the world. The boom is remembered as "The Glory Days."

A Good Place to Watch a Bullfight

Wilburn Cross is an expert at calling animals. He can stand in the woods around his house near Atlanta, Texas, and call up deer, fox, raccoon, turkey, bobcat, and other types of wildlife. Wilburn doesn't use any mechanical device. He uses only his mouth.

He has been known to walk in a grocery store and meow like a cat. Customers all over the store would look for it. Wilburn just loves to fool people that way.

He can sound like a frog, a dog, a hog, a horse, a mule, or just about any other four-legged creature. He says he learned how to do it by just listening to the animals.

He makes bird sounds, too. Owls are his specialty. He occasionally will explore an owl's nest. "Boy, you've never had a scrappin' 'til you try to look in an owl's nest," says Wilburn. "They'll sure getcha. They'll tear you up. Until an owl is older, he's completely white. Then he'll feather out and turn owl-colored. Hawks and buzzards are the same way. They're snow white until they feather out."

When Wilburn drives into downtown Atlanta, he usually brings his pet roosters along. He leaves them around his pickup while he goes into the drugstore, barbershop, or post office. Wilburn's pickup with roosters resting on it is a common sight around Atlanta. "See, they're familiar with that old pickup. Everything in town is new to them, but that pickup is like their home. So they won't run off. Every once in a while the town noises will set them off crowin'. Some people like them, others don't. Some people walkin' by act like they're scared to death of my roosters."

One time Wilburn was visiting his father-in-law and went out to take a walk. He stopped when he got to a fence separating his father-in-law's place from a ranch owned by a man named Ed Peel.

Wilburn got the urge to call up something. So he climbed up a redbud tree and looked around. He saw a bull.

"I commenced making a bull sound," says Wilburn. "In a minute, here comes this bull just a runnin'. Now, old Ed Peel had a good fence there. It was web wire at the bottom and three strands of barbed wire on top of it. It was a strong fence. That bull hit that fence and it just came apart. He just tore it all down. That bull came over to that redbud tree and started pawing dirt. Man, he was mad. And I was keepin' him upset by bawlin' and bellerin' like a bull. I wanted to keep him there so he wouldn't run off. He tore that ground up. He'd butt that tree and it would shake me. But I knew he couldn't shove that tree down."

In a minute or two, a bull belonging to Wilburn's daddy-in-law trotted over, wanting to see what all the commotion was about.

"My daddy-in-law's bull started bellerin' then. Boy, he was upset. Those two bulls started mixing it up, and brother, you have never seen such a bullfight. They'd hit that tree I was in and I'd have to hold on for dear life. Leaves and sticks from that tree just peppered down. Those two bulls fought till they were wringin' wet with sweat. I don't know which one was declared the winner. They both just got so tired they quit fightin', and one went one way and one went the other."

Wilburn climbed down from the tree and went back to the house and told his father-in-law that there had been a big bull-fight and Ed Peel's fence was torn down. Wilburn's father-in-law called Ed Peel, and they agreed to meet at the place where the fence was damaged.

"Old Ed showed up with some barbed wire, and the three of us fixed the fence. They wanted to pay me for helping, but I told them they didn't owe me anything. They never did find out who caused that bullfight."

The Bird Lady of Wildwood

Mary Reed lives in a little place called Wildwood south of Woodville. It is a small resort community built around a creek-fed lake and an eighteen-hole golf course. Tall pines grace the landscape.

While Mary was a teacher, she became interested in birds. "When the kids studied things from nature they seemed more interested," says Mary. She put bird feeders just outside the classroom windows, and the children became accustomed to seeing different types of birds.

She says to be a bird watcher you need two things: a good

bird book and a good pair of binoculars. She uses the *Golden Guide to Birds of North America,* because she likes the way the groupings are done. It also has a chart that explains bird calls.

Mary conducts classes to teach people how to become bird watchers. She never charges for her services. "It's more fun that way," says Mary.

She has filing cabinets full of letters from people who attended her bird-watching classes. Most of the letters tell her how their lives had been changed for the better since they became bird watchers.

Her backyard is full of things for birds. She even had her husband plant a dead tree where the birds can perch. Three birdbaths have water dripping into them. "It's always best to have some movement in their water. It attracts more birds." She has a single piece of copper tubing coming out of a faucet next to each birdbath. It extends upward, makes a rainbow curve, and drips into the birdbath.

Mary doesn't put out birdseed in the summer months. "Natural food is better for them, and there are so many natural things out there." She hangs a concoction of suet, peanut butter, oatmeal, birdseed, and syrup in the trees during winter months.

She observes how birds sleep. "They have a trigger mechanism in their feet. When they go to sleep on a branch of a tree, their feet lock around the branch. That way, they won't fall while they're sleeping."

She likes bird watching because it gets her outside. "Then when I'm outside, I can't help but notice the flowers, trees, plants, and other things in nature. Besides, it's an activity you can do with friends."

Last year she put up houses for bluebirds and established a bluebird trail. "We built seventy-three houses and put them up around Wildwood, mostly in people's backyards. We raised 149 birds. We kept thorough notes on the project." These are the eastern variety of bluebirds, about the size of a sparrow.

The other day a neighbor went to Mary's house carrying a small bluebird in a cloth. It had flown into a window. Mary's husband held the bird for a while in his hands and talked to it. He noticed every once in a while the bird would open its

SITE OF

MARY ALLEN SEMINARY

IN 1886 THE BOARD OF MISSIONS FOR FREEDMEN OF THE PRESBYTERIAN CHURCH IN THE UNITED STATES, UNDER THE LEADERSHIP OF THE GROUP'S SECRETARY THE REV. RICHARD ALLEN, BEGAN PLANNING FOR THE ESTABLISHMENT OF A BLACK GIRLS' SCHOOL IN TEXAS. AFTER A STATEWIDE SURVEY, THEY CHOSE CROCKETT AS THE SCHOOL SITE BECAUSE OF THE AREA'S LARGE BLACK POPULATION AND BECAUSE OF A LOCAL BLACK PAROCHIAL SCHOOL OPERATED BY THE REV. SAMUEL FISHER TENNEY, PASTOR OF THE CITY'S FIRST PRESBYTERIAN CHURCH. THE REV. ALLEN'S WIFE MARY, FOR WHOM THE SCHOOL WAS NAMED, WAS INSTRUMENTAL IN RAISING THE ORGANIZATIONAL FUNDS FOR THE NEW SEMINARY.

DR. BYRD R. SMITH BECAME THE SCHOOL'S FIRST BLACK PRESIDENT IN 1924 AND INITIATED A PERIOD OF GROWTH WHICH INCLUDED THE ADOPTION OF NEW PROGRAMS AND THE ADMISSION OF MALE STUDENTS. TRANSFERRED TO THE MISSIONARY GENERAL BAPTIST CONVENTION OF TEXAS IN 1944, MARY ALLEN COLLEGE BECAME A 4-YEAR LIBERAL ARTS INSTITUTION. IN 1972, PLAGUED BY A SERIES OF LEGAL AND FINANCIAL SETBACKS, THE SCHOOL CLOSED.

ONCE THE SITE OF A 12-BUILDING CAMPUS AND THE HOME OF A NOTED ACADEMIC PROGRAM OF QUALITY EDUCATION AND RELIGION, THIS SITE SERVES AS A REMINDER OF THE PROUD HERITAGE OF TEXAS' BLACK POPULATION.

(1982)

eyes. In less than an hour the bird was feeling better and flew up to a ceiling fan. Mary's husband thought it was fully recovered, so he went outside to release it. Outside, the little bird uttered a cry as it flew to the nearest limb. Within five seconds there were two bluebirds on either side of the little bird. In another five seconds, three other bluebirds had come in to check out the situation. They huddled around the little bird to check it out and see if it was all right. The birds stayed there about eight minutes, then flew off together.

"The bluebirds are here all the time," says Mary. "We might not see them, but they're here." She calls her place a bluebird paradise. Her house has a large picture window that allows her to look out into her backyard. She designed her house so she could watch the birds even while cooking. "When company comes, we watch the birds. Even non-bird watchers get involved. Along with the birds, we have eleven squirrels that come to play. There's never a dull moment."

The Folklore of Overalls

Charles Horchem ranches north of Winnsboro in Northeast Texas. He is the proud owner of five pairs of overalls. He saves his best and newest pair to wear on Sundays. When he's working with cows during the week, he wears old ones.

"If you raise cotton, you wear blue overalls," he says. "If you're a carpenter, mechanic, or work on the railroad, you wear striped ones. If you raise cows, you wear blue ones with white stripes. On Sunday, you wear white ones with blue stripes on them."

He says if you're scared of lightning, twist the shoulder straps on the overalls and lightning won't strike you.

Some people go around with just one strap fastened. "Those folks are just too lazy to hook 'em up," says Charles. "But if you're playing with a yo-yo, whichever hand you have that yo-yo in, you undo that strap. That makes it easier and the strap don't ride down on your shoulder. It's more comfortable yo-yoing that way."

He says size is real important in wearing overalls. "If you wear a size 38 blue jeans, the smallest overalls you can wear is size 40. And you really need them 42 so air can come up the britches leg and cool you off. If you wear them real tight, you don't get any ventilation.

One thing he likes about overalls is you don't have to wear a belt and you don't have to keep pulling your pants up. Overalls stay up.

Overalls have buttons on the side. "Those are for expansion," says Charles. "If you expand too much, you can take a rubber band and slip through that hole and it'll hook right over that button."

He likes all the pockets and compartments on overalls. "You've got a place for your watch and your pencil, your pliers and hammer and measuring stick. You can carry lots of stuff when you wear overalls."

He debunks the various theories and legends about wearing the pants leg of your overalls inside your boots. "Everybody says if you own so many cows you put one britches leg in your boots, and if you own a lot more cattle you put both pants legs inside your boots. That's all baloney. You wear your britches leg in the boots so you don't get anything on 'em. Then if you have to go to town you take them out and they cover that manure you've got all over your boots. You can go in the store and get something and nobody looks bad at you."

He says the only time you roll up your britches leg is when you wade out to get a calf out of a pool of water. "It may look silly wearing your overall pants like that, but you look silly anyway getting that calf out of the water."

Old folks used to buy overalls because they were cheap, but Charles says they're pretty expensive now. "You've got to have a pretty good income to wear new ones."

He says Big Smith and Roundhouse brands of overalls last a long time. "A pair will last about five years."

When some people are putting on a pair of overalls and

try to flip the straps over, the metal fasteners on the end sometimes hit them on the head. But Charles says that's okay. "You're hardheaded or you wouldn't be ranching, so it don't hurt."

He says you should never iron overalls. "They'd look funny with a crease in them. Just wash them and hang them out on the line to dry. When they're dry, shake them a few times and they'll be ready to wear."

He says you don't see many people under forty years old wearing overalls, but there's a reason for that. "Overalls are for working people. People under forty don't take work very serious."

He says overalls go back in history a long time. "I think the pilgrims had overalls. They were probably black. I think there was one old boy with Moses that had a pair."

The Origin of the Hamburger

Athens is the third county seat of Henderson County. The previous ones were Buffalo and Centerville. Athens used to be called Alfred, named for the city's first postmaster, Alfred Mallard. "There was a lady named Dulcette Averitt, and she is credited with naming Athens," says Gayle Davis. "She named it after Athens, Greece, thinking one day Athens would be the cultural center of Henderson County."

One historical group in Athens says the city was named for Athens, Alabama, where the Averitt family originated.

Athens claims to be the home of the hamburger. "In 1904, at the St. Louis World's Fair, a gentlemen by the name of Fletcher Davis originated the hamburger," says Gayle. "In the late 1800s he had a cafe on the downtown square in Athens which served a sandwich consisting of ground meat, a thick slice of Bermuda onion, and a mustard mixture that he put between two homemade buns. The citizens of Athens were so impressed with his sandwich, they decided to send him to the World's Fair in St. Louis. It was there Fletcher Davis introduced his sandwich to the world and it became known as the hamburger."

Athens celebrates the hamburger annually by staging the Uncle Fletch Davis Memorial World Hamburger Cook-Off. During the first cook-off in 1984, a historical marker was unveiled on the site of Fletch's cafe.

The event is divided into different categories. "There's one for backyard chefs, which are considered amateurs," says Gayle. "Then we have one for professional restaurateurs."

The event, staged in the spring, attracts a number of star athletes and well-known Texas personalities.

Athens is famous for another food item, the black-eyed

pea. Henderson County produces tons of them every year in its sandy soil. The vegetable is on most menus in East Texas. In 1971 Athens residents were trying to come up with some type of county-wide celebration. They looked around at what was most obvious and decided to have a Black-Eyed Pea Jamboree. There was a cannery in Athens at the time which canned black-eyed peas, so it helped get the event started. It's been going strong ever since.

The cannery helped advertise the July event by sending cans of black-eyed peas to newsrooms across the country. The cannery's public relations department sent them to reporters in late December every year to remind them of the Texas tradition of eating black-eyed peas on New Year's Day for good luck.

During the festival, a Miss Black-Eyed Pea is crowned, and there are contests to determine who can shell the most peas within a given time, or who can pop the peas out of the shell the most distance. Judges from all over the country go to Athens to judge food prepared from what are called ReciPEAS.

Both the Black-Eyed Pea Jamboree and the Hamburger Cook-Off take a back seat to another event in Athens. The Texas Fiddler's Contest and Reunion, held the last Friday in May, is more than fifty years old and attracts people from all over the U.S. and beyond.

Henderson County historian Jana Shumate says that during the 1960s Henderson County had more millionaires per capita than anywhere else in the U.S. John Wayne, Willie Nelson, and Waylon Jennings all had ranches or farms in Henderson County. Two of the county's more famous wealthy men were Sid Richardson and Clint Murchison.

Cotton Fields

Jean Morris of Lake Palestine grew up in Athens. In 1936 she spent some time on the Bluebird Ranch near Wilma, Texas. The ranch was owned by Clint Murchison, an Athens boy who made good.

"I had a little Shetland Pony named Old Paint," says Jean. "I rode it all over the ranch. It was really a beautiful place."

One area of the ranch was like an old southern plantation, with acres of cotton fields. "I used to ride down there and watch the blacks in the fields, working," says Jean. "It was like watching the movie *Gone With The Wind*. There was so much music and rhythm in the people as they went from row to row picking the cotton.

"Way over in one part of the field a voice would explode in song. Then way back on the other side someone else would join in. Then someone in the middle of the field would pick up the tune. Soon there was singing all over that acreage. People would absolutely drive around from time to time in their automobiles and wagons just to hear them sing. They were singing the old spirituals.

"My uncle, who was the foreman of the ranch, would be on his horse, and he would have two helpers, and they would ride around and check the cotton, see what was being brought in, what was being picked, how long it took them to do it. And these people would literally stay out there from the morning until the late evening to get the cotton picked. It was amazing to me that they were all ages. Little children with their mothers would work alongside each other. Everybody was busy picking cotton.

"I never heard a complaint from any of them. They seemed to be so happy. That's the thing that struck my heart the most.

"Some of those people who were singing in the cotton fields back in 1936 sounded better than today's superstars. And it was a joy to see the joy in them. I'm glad I was able to see that culture at that time."

Directions

When I'm driving out of town I sometimes get lost. I have been lost on caliche roads that lead to somebody's barnyard. I've also been lost in the middle of large cities.

Stopping to ask directions is always an adventure. You learn a lot about the area where you are. When someone gives me directions and closes his comments with the phrase "You can't miss it," I always miss it.

I was looking for Motel 6 in Longview the other day and stopped to ask a man how to get there. His answer proved to me that he knew quite a bit about his city. The next paragraphs are the words of his reply.

"I tell you what you do. Okay. Here's the way you gotta go. Okay. You get to this yield sign, right? You go down to that first light right there. Okay. You go through that first light. Okay. When you get to the second light, it's an intersection. One way goin' this way, one way goin' straight through like this, and another way just goes straight period. It's a tricky intersection. Okay.

"When you get to that second light, you take that bend. That'd be to the left. All right. You come to a library. To the left. Another light. At the end of that light, okay, between where you take the bend at, the library and the police station is to the left, gonna pass by the police station, Longview police, pass by the library and then you gonna come to another light at the end of that street. Okay. Then at the end of that street is an Exxon station to the right 'Cross the street from the Exxon station is Kilgore Junior College. 'Cross over here is a car lot. Right over here is a finance company. Okay. You take a right, right there at that light. Keep it straight. Keep it straight. Bam.

"You come to another light right after you pass the college. When it turns green, bam. You come to another light. You keep it straight. You go on over a bridge. Okay. When you go on over that bridge, bam.

"You come to another light. There's a YMCA to the right. They have a new place they just put up, I think it's a Payless

Cashway, shoe store or something. You go on through that. Bam.

"Come to another light. They got Brookshire's. Right across the street they got a 7-11. Right across the street they got a Payless Cashway. Right turn on green, you leave that light. You go to another light. Bam.

"On to another light. There's a Texaco. Right there to the right. Biggest Texaco in Longview. Right there to the right. That light turn green, you leave that light. Bam.

"You come to another light. There's a Winn-Dixie over there. Shoppin' Center. Big ol' Winn-Dixie. Marathon LeTourneau, one of the biggest refineries in Longview, is right there.

They got five big ol' domes. They build bombs there. Okay. When you leave that light, you keep it straight. Bam.

"You come to another light. Come to another light. They got a store across the street, they got a lawnmower place across the street, to the left they got a lawnmower shop and then they got a gas company right there. Eastex Gas Company. Then they got a store across the street and they got another store across the street right there. You go on through that light. Bam. You come to a place down there they got a La Quinta Inn. Okay, after you leave La Quinta Inn they got a light at La Quinta Inn. You take that first right. At La Quinta Inn. They got some kinda little restaurant there, you get all you can eat for $4. You take that right there at that light and there's the Motel 6."

I love stopping and asking for directions. I always learn a lot.

A Bridge Crossing to Remember

The Roberts family earned a lot of money in 1936 and decided to return to their home state of Alabama for a visit. James Roberts says his grandmother hadn't been back there since 1898.

"We carried my grandmother and my uncle plus five kids and Mother and Daddy. You couldn't get them all in a four-door Plymouth, so we pulled a two-wheeled trailer and put hoops and a tarp over it like a covered wagon. My two younger brothers and I rode in the trailer all the way to Alabama."

James's father loved history, and each time the family stopped to eat, he told them what a magnificent experience it was going to be to cross the Mississippi River at Memphis, Tennessee.

About ten miles before they got to the bridge over the mighty river, a tire blew out on the trailer. There was no spare, so James's father and an uncle took a cedar post from a fence alongside the highway and slung it under that right wheel.

James said they took baling wire and made the cedar post secure against the wheel. "We had a tire on one side and a fence post on the other. And we had a five-gallon can of water, and my brother and I had a special job. We leaned out the back of that trailer, and when that fence post caught fire we'd pour water on it. Smoke was coming out of that cedar post, you wouldn't believe it. We could go about a hundred yards before it would catch on fire, then we'd pour water on it. My older brother was holding my feet and I was leaning out the back of the trailer to make sure the water got in the right spot."

By the time they got to the bridge, traffic was backed up for five miles and a steady stream of smoke and water was coming out the back of that trailer. "We crossed the Mississippi River, and I was so busy putting out the fire that I never got to see the river."

Shoes

A man in East Texas likes shoes. He has saved all the shoes he bought for his kids while they were growing up. He could make a line of shoes a block long.

This man also has a mule that lives in a small steel building behind his house. The building once served as the jail in Joaquin, Texas.

That building is one of half a dozen structures scattered over four acres of land right in town where this man lives. His home is filled with things he enjoys: his pocketknife collection, his colorful arrowhead collection, and his clock collection. A gigantic grandfather clock sits in his foyer.

One of his buildings contains nothing but Fashion clocks. The Fashion Clockworks made some classic clocks years ago, and he has at least one of every model they sold.

This man also collects old end tables. He has one or more of them in each of his buildings.

What he is keeping in the structures is simply stuff that means a lot to him. He grew up with some of the items. Others he acquired over the years. He has an old undertaker's bag that belonged to the founder of a funeral home in town.

He has furniture and equipment from an old dentist's office. He even has an old machine from a beauty shop that once gave women permanents. He has several saddles from men he admired and respected while he was growing up.

This man has a green thumb. His four acres are covered with bushes, trees, flowers, and a garden. The tall pine trees were once little seedlings that he transported from the woods in small buckets. A grapevine he planted years ago now swings from tree to tree high off the ground.

His azaleas are something to behold in the spring, and his cantaloupes, peaches, apples, and pears have a sweet taste.

This man has a full, rich life. He has family and friends, things he enjoys, loves where he lives, and owns a profitable business.

But even today, there are things about his youth that still bother him. Things that explain why shoes mean so much to him. He asked me not to use his real name if I repeated the following story he told me. I'll refer to him as Charlie.

Charlie grew up poor. He was hungry a good portion of his youth. Every day was a struggle. His family worked hard.

When he started to school he didn't have any shoes, so he wore a pair that belonged to his mother. The students ridiculed him. Laughed at him. Charlie was humiliated.

Later on, he became friends with a boy whose father was a jailer in the courthouse. The jailer and his wife cooked for the prisoners and lived on the premises. Charlie was in high school, but still didn't have any decent shoes to wear. One night he and his friend went to the courthouse. The friend wanted to show him something.

There had been a raid on a gambling den, and the lawmen had confiscated a nickel slot machine. It was in the courthouse, near the jail. His friend turned the slot machine upside down, and nickels began to pour from it. They whooped and hollered and scooped up handfuls of nickels.

In all, three dollars and twenty cents worth of nickels had fallen out of the slot machine. They agreed to split the money evenly. But the jailer's son looked down at his buddy's worn out shoes and gave him his half of the money and said, "Why-don't you go to the store tomorrow and buy yourself some new shoes." Charlie did. And from that day, his fortune seemed to change.

Years later, when Charlie was grown and successful, he bought an expensive pair of boots for his friend who had given him money to buy his first new pair of shoes. That friend appreciated those boots and died wearing them.

General East Texas Info

Grand Saline has a visitor information center built of salt blocks, the only one of its kind in the U.S. A secondary fiber-glass roof protects it from rain and weather. Grand Saline has a huge salt dome, mined by Morton Salt Company since 1929. All types of salt, from the table variety to rock salt for ice cream, are produced in Grand Saline.

Greenville is the birthplace of World War II hero Audie Murphy. Greenville also has a steam cotton compress that was once the world's largest inland press and held the record for the number of cotton bales compressed in one day: 2,073.

Henderson has the only outhouse in Texas with a histori-cal marker. It is a three-holer built in 1908.

Kaufman's first courthouse was in a remodeled black-smith shop.

Kilgore had so many oil derricks on one city block, work-ers walked on planks high in the air between them.

Longview got its name from railroad surveyors who ex-claimed when they arrived there, "Wow, look at the long view."

Lufkin has the state's only forestry museum.

Mabank was named after its two founders, Dodge Mason and Tom Eubank.

Marshall, Texas, served as the capital of Missouri during the Civil War.

Mineola was called Sodom until 1873, when Ira Evans named it for his daughter Minnie and her best friend, Ola.

Nacogdoches is called the oldest town in Texas because El Camino Real, now a main city thoroughfare, was cut through the dense forests in the 1700s to establish trade with the Indians. Burial mounds in the area date back to 1250 A.D.

Rusk has the longest footbridge in the U.S.

Sulphur Springs, known for its sulfur springs, was first called Bright Star.

Wills Point is named for the town's founder, William Wills.

I've visited the East Texas villages of Bump, Nose, Two-Egg, and Hot. Dr. Fred Tarpley, who studies Texas place names, says no other state has as many fascinating names for communities as Texas. He studies rural school names. "Sometimes they had a box supper and an auction to raise funds. They would name the school for the young lady whose food brought the greatest amount of money. When a school was already named, the community that would grow up around it would be named the same as the school."

The name Salem pops up all over the place. "It's a shortening of Jerusalem, with biblical significance," says Fred. Mars Hill, Jerico, and Ebenezer are other biblical names appearing quite frequently over the East Texas countryside. Mount Mariah and Mount Hebron are also from the Bible."

Grover Dye's Tall Tale

When I visited with Grover Dye in Woodville, he was popping a whip. The loud explosions from the tip of the whip echoed through the forest. His daddy had a bull skinner's whip.

"Now, a bull skinner's whip is about ten feet long with a double stock," says Grover. "That's a piece of hickory wood made into a good stock about three feet long."

His daddy was a logger.

"One day when I was a little boy, my dad used a team of oxen that consisted of five yokes. That's ten head to an eight-wheel log wagon. Once he was logging way back up in the woods close to a boggy branch. My mother told me to take lunch to him, that he wasn't coming in for lunch that day.

"When I got up there close to where he was working, I could hear him just a-hollerin' and poppin' that whip. As I got on up to him, I saw he was standing there on the bank of that boggy branch poppin' that whip and there wasn't a single thing in sight. No wagon, no oxen or anything.

"So I sat down there beside him for a little bit. I noticed him becoming more excited, more rushed. It seemed like he was trying to hurry up. He would yell out, 'Whoa, whoa, Ball.'

"The head ox was named Ball. Others were named Rock and Jerry. If they can hear you, they're supposed to come to you, if they're trained. And my dad's oxen were sure trained, 'cause they got lots of work out there in the woods.

"He kept hollerin', 'Whoa, Ball, whoa, Jerry!' That means come here. He kept shoutin', 'Whoa, Rock, come on outa there.'

"Finally I got his attention and asked him what he was doin'. I thought he was crazy standing there poppin' that whip and yellin' down into the mud like that.

"He said, 'Son, I was going back to the woods empty while ago with these oxen, and Ball was so thirsty when they crossed that boggy branch bridge, they just fell off the end of it and headed down to the water to get a drink of water. The lead pair went in the water, then the next and the next. After a while they were all down there, buried in that mud.'

"I said, 'Papa, you're not serious.' He said he was. 'But if they ever hear me, they'll be coming out of there. But they've got to do it within a few minutes or they'll suffocate down there.'

"So he took in a long breath, a real deep one, crawled up on a bigger stump, and popped that whip and hollered just as

loud as he could. The voice was so loud, the echo just show-
ered the acorns off those trees all around that forest.

"After a while I noticed two horns coming out of that
mud. Then came two more, and the next and the next. Pretty
soon all four yoke of oxen were out on that bank and we were
wiping the mud and slush out of their nostrils and eyes so they
could breathe and see.

"I told Papa I thought he had told me the wagon was
empty when it went into the water. He said it was and then
asked, 'What's that on it?'

"We pulled it out there on the bank, and there was a catfish lodged on that log wagon. It had apparently been down in
that mud for a long time. It was sixty-six feet and thirteen
inches long.

"And we gave a big catfish fry for all the residents of Polk
and Tyler counties. We didn't eat over half that fish. It was
some kinda big."

Square Dancing

Square dancing is an American folk dance that is multi-
cultural. It has evolved from Slavic, Scandinavian, African,
European, Middle Eastern, and Asian influences.

It has its origins in rural areas, where people take pride in
preserving their heritage and culture.

The soul of a people manifests itself in the celebration of
festive occasions. The dances represent custom and tradition
and lend dignity and substance to the life of its people.

Square dancing is the ideal foreign relationship. An
Irishman can enjoy a dance with a Greek. I heard a man from
Scotland say: "You can't fight a man you've danced with."

Square dancing reflects the American soul, which is of
mixed ancestry, descended from immigrants who came to this
country's shores from many lands. The dance carries with it
the character and spirit of the American pioneers.

The spicy western calls, the New England singing and

quadrilles, the elaborate and beautiful Texas Star Dances, the vigorous double couple dances of the Southern Appalachians all contribute to the overall fabric of today's modern square dance.

The music long ago might have come from a fiddle, banjo, guitar, accordion, fife, drum, or hand clapping. Today's callers travel with their own customized sound systems, playing recorded music and using a microphone. And even though the dancers might speak another language, the calls are always in English.

Square dancing has become popular because of the glowing smiles on the faces of the dancers. People want something to smile about. Young or old, city or country, elaborately dressed or in everyday clothes, square dancing is fun.

Dancers are rewarded with new friendships, mental relaxation, and feelings of social well being. Stag lines, wallflowers and self-consciousness are forgotten when the caller yells, "Square your sets!"

The terms *do-si-do, promenade,* and *allemande* signify a good time. Square dancing is a dance of friendship.

Several couples dancing complex patterns such as stars, chains and cloverleaves, create a tapestry of swirling color and rhythm. The dancers move to the beat of the haunting music and the caller's chant. They express their appreciation of life. The dance itself is an expression of joy.

There is no folk without folk dances.

Young children can square dance. So can their grandparents. And they can dance in the same set. Blind and partially crippled people have been taught to square dance and gain a real sense of accomplishment. It teaches youngsters social behavior.

Some communities block off streets and have summertime dances outdoors.

When dancers do a square from New England, Texas, or Minnesota, they absorb the flavor of the regional calls and movements and somehow gain the feeling of knowing New Englanders, Texans, and Minnesotans just a little bit better.

Swinging your partner is a good way to keep the blood circulating. Calico prints, crinoline petticoats, boots, and bandanas represent people who are interested in physical condi-

tioning, personality development, and gaining an awareness of the nation's culture.

Volunteerism, sincerity, friendliness, dedication, and fun. They're all important ingredients of square dancing.

East Texas Music

East Texans couldn't survive without music. In the early days, music meant fun times, a chance to take a break from the hard work of making a living from the land. When someone started playing a fiddle, the worries of the day seemed to disappear and people relaxed. They were ready to visit with friends and party.

Music was played mostly for dances in those early days. Rooms would be cleared of furniture, and those on hand would dance to the music of local players. Most of the musicians were fellow farmers who played as a sideline for a modest sum—usually whatever cash was brought in when the hat was passed.

Most of the time there was just fiddle and guitar, but sometimes other stringed instruments, such as mandolin and banjo, would join in. Traveling tent shows brought musical entertainment to the rural areas.

Most early singers got their start by singing hymns in church. Singing teachers taught mostly by the shaped note system, which uses symbols rather than standard musical notes to indicate the pitch of the tone. One version, the "sacred harp" singing, is still heard in parts of East Texas.

"Sallie Gooden" and "Arkansas Traveler" were popular fiddle tunes in the 1920s. In 1923 radio station WBAP in Fort Worth started a "barn dance"–type radio show that helped popularize country music. The Aladdin Laddies and the Light Crust Doughboys were musical groups that became famous due to their performances on radio.

Southerners who settled in East Texas brought their slaves with them. The African Americans sang as they worked long, hot hours on farms and plantations, reflecting a style of music called the blues. Black musicians sometimes played for whites, who listened or danced. Henry "Ragtime Texas" Thomas, born in Gladewater in 1875, performed blues music with his voice, guitar, and panpipe when he was in his fifties.

Mance Lipscomb, born near Navasota in 1895, worked most of his life as a sharecropper, singing blues, ballads, dance tunes, and religious songs. He was discovered by the folk music crowd in the 1960s and enjoyed considerable popularity during the last years of his life.

Another significant musical figure was Huddie Ledbetter, who was known as "Leadbelly." He was born in 1889 on the shores of Caddo Lake. He spent much of his time in Texas when he wasn't in prison. He popularized the song "Goodnight, Irene."

Leadbelly used a twelve-string guitar as his primary instrument. He learned much about the blues from Blind Lemon Jefferson, who became the first country blues recording star. He was born in 1893 in the Couchman community, about an hour south of Dallas. Jefferson walked the roads around his home, playing for money on streets and in cafes and joints. He spent some time in Mexia, where a strip of black businesses was known as the Beat, playing both alone and in a string band with other musicians.

Bob Wills, who developed country swing, was born in 1905 and spent the first years of his life at Kosse, not far from Couchman. Chances are he heard Blind Lemon Jefferson and Marlin's Blind Willie Johnson, who played guitar and sang gospel blues.

Blind Lemon Jefferson became a popular recording star and spent a lot of time in Chicago and Dallas. His music achieved success in the "race" market, records marketed exclusively to blacks. He recorded a few spirituals under the name Deacon L. J. Bates.

Jefferson's recording success opened the door to a flood of country blues recordings by artists such as "Little Hat" Jones, Alger "Texas" Alexander, and J. T. "Funny Papa" Smith. The music style of these pioneers was a major influence on T-Bone Walker and other blues players who started playing electric guitars in the mid 1930s. Thus the guitar became a solo instrument instead of being part of the rhythm section of a large band.

An earthier strain of blues was exemplified by Sam "Lightnin'" Hopkins of Centerville, who spent much of his time in Houston playing an amplified version of the East Texas music he heard as a child.

Texas had a strong tradition of piano blues, too, popularized by composers such as Scott Joplin, who developed his music in the rough lumber and turpentine camps of East Texas. He played in Dallas's Deep Ellum district and in Houston nightspots like Mud Alley and The Vamp.

In the 1950s, urban blues sprang up in the Don Robey's Duke and Peacock Studios in Houston. Artists in this genre included Clarence "Gatemouth" Brown, Bobby "Blue" Bland, and Willie Mae "Big Mama" Thornton, whose recording of "Hound Dog" inspired Elvis Presley.

In 1925 Dallas's Tip Top dance hall featured local clarinetist and alto sax player Henry "Buster" Smith, who toured with a jazz band called the Blue Devils. He helped establish Kansas City's jazz scene and helped create Count Basie's "One O'Clock Jump." Smith had a big influence on Charlie Parker, known as the father of bebop.

Cindy Walker of Mexia achieved success as both a songwriter and singer. She wrote "Dream Baby" for Roy Orbison, "You Don't Know Me" for Eddie Arnold, and several songs for Bob Wills, including "Cherokee Maiden," "Dusty Skies," and "Bubbles in My Beer." She appeared in movies with Gene Autry, and her song "When My Blue Moon Turns to Gold Again" was a Top 10 hit in 1944. Cindy Walker was the first woman inducted into the Nashville Songwriters Hall of Fame.

One of East Texas' most famous musical performers was Janis Joplin, born in Port Arthur. She grew up listening to black blues singers. While attending the University of Texas at Austin, she started singing at Kenneth Threadgills' nightclub before migrating to California, where she sang folk songs in hippie joints. She went on to became a national star.

A list of East Texas artists and hometowns:

Vernon Dalhart   Jefferson   Country-Western

Al Dexter	Troup	Country-Western
Ernest Tubb	Crisp	Country-Western
Johnny Horton	Tyler	Country-Western
Lefty Frizzel	Corsicana	Country-Western
Ray Price	Perryville	Country-Western
George Jones	Saratoga	Country-Western
Jim Reeves	Carthage	Country-Western
Tex Ritter	Carthage	Country-Western
T-Bone Walker	Linden	Blues
Harry James	Beaumont	Trumpet Player
Don Henley	Linden	Singer with the Eagles

San Jacinto: No Small Affair

For some reason, the Alamo gets publicity, and Texans are constantly reminded of a lost battle. In comparison, the San Jacinto battlefield is only seldom mentioned, yet it is at San Jacinto that Texas won its independence from Mexico. San Jacinto, twenty-two miles southeast of Houston, is a nice place to visit. Huge oak trees grace the old battleground, which is now a 445-acre state park. A reflecting pool is on the premises.

The most imposing monument in the state is here. It is an art deco shaft that stands 570 feet high—fifteen feet higher than the Washington Monument. It commemorates the heroes of the Battle of San Jacinto and all other people who helped win independence for Texas.

The San Jacinto Monument was built by the Works Progress Administration between 1936 and 1939 at a cost of $1.5 million. It was erected because somebody thought Texas ought to have something to mark the state's 100th birthday. The limestone walls are studded with Texas fossils. An account of the battle is engraved on the four sides of the base. An interior elevator takes sightseers to the top for a view of the Houston Ship Channel. Adults ride for $1.50; children pay 50¢.

The base is forty-eight feet square and tapers to thirty

square feet at the observation tower. A star thirty-four feet high tops the monument. On the bronze doors of the building are reliefs of the six flags of Texas.

The monument has a small museum which traces the history of the area. Next to the monument is the battleship *Texas*, which saw action in two world wars.

The San Jacinto is a short river, running about eighty-five miles to the gulf through Galveston Bay. Two stories prevail as to how the river was named. One is that when explorers first saw it, the river was choked with hyacinth (*acinto* in Spanish). The other is that it was discovered on St. Hyacinth's Day, August 17.

It was on the shore of the San Jacinto that the Battle of San Jacinto was fought on April 21, 1836.

The battle was the concluding military event of the Texas Revolution. It took place about 3:30 in the afternoon. The Texans, led by Sam Houston, attacked while Santa Anna and his troops were taking a siesta. The battle lasted only eighteen minutes. Texans attacked from three sides, with cries of "Remember the Alamo! Remember Goliad!" The enemy was forced to retreat into the water.

Houston's casualty report listed 630 Mexicans killed and 730 taken prisoner. Only 39 of the 910 Texans were killed or wounded. Houston's ankle was shattered by a cannonball. Santa Anna escaped during the battle but was recaptured the next day.

One of the inscriptions on the base of the San Jacinto Monument reads: "Measured by its results, San Jacinto was one of the decisive battles of the world. The freedom of Texas from Mexico won here led to the acquisition by the United States of the states of Texas, New Mexico, Arizona, Nevada, California, Utah and parts of Colorado, Wyoming, Kansas, and Oklahoma. Almost one-third of the present area of the American nation, nearly a million square miles of territory, changed sovereignty."

Bibliography

Books

Abernethy, Francis Edward, ed. *Built in Texas*. Denton, Texas: University of North Texas Press, 200.

Bishop, Eliza. "First County of the Republic of Texas." Houston County Historical Society, 1980.

Dahmer, Fred. *Caddo Was: A Short History of Caddo Lake*. Austin, Texas: University of Texas Press, 1995.

Elder, Jack, and Caleb Pirtle III. *The Glory Days*. Austin, Texas: Nortex Press, 1986.

Fehrenbach, T. R. *Lone Star: A History of Texas and the Texians*. New York: Da Capo Press, 2000.

Jack, William. *Gaston High School, Joinerville, Texas*.

Johnson, Jerry. *County Scrapbook*. New York: Simon and Schuster, 1977.

Kent, Rosemary. *Genuine Texas Handbook*. New York: Workman Publishing, 1981.

King, Lincoln, Sierra McGarity, and Cassie Downing. *Loblolly Looks at Panola County*. Gary, Texas: Loblolly Press, 1998.

Ramos, Mary G., ed. *Texas Almanac*. Dallas, Texas: Dallas Morning News, 1997.

Rosser, Howard W. *East Texas Vacation Guide*. East Texas Chamber of Commerce publication.

Tarpley, Fred. *1001 Texas Place Names*. Austin, Texas: University of Texas Press, 1980.

Texas History Movies. Texas Educational Association, 1974.

Articles

Bishop, Eliza. *First County of the Republic of Texas*. Texas: Houston County Historical Society 1980.

About the Author

Tumbleweed Smith is producer of *The Sound of Texas,* a radio series which began in Big Spring and became the most widely syndicated radio show in Texas. In doing his daily program for more than thirty years, he has gathered the largest private collection of oral history in the United States.

Texas Highways magazine says he has probably recorded more Texas characters on tape than anyone else.

He has taught broadcasting at the University of Texas of the Permian Basin since 1974. He is a syndicated newspaper columnist. His one-man show, *Texas Stories,* is part of the Texas Commission on the Arts Touring Arts Program. He graduated from Baylor with a degree in English, has a master's degree in journalism from the University of Missouri, and studied law at Drake University.

He owns an advertising and production company and has won international recognition for his work. His honors include the Governor's Award for Tourism, the West Texas Chamber of Commerce Cultural Achievement Award, and two Freedoms Foundation Awards.

He is a past district governor of Rotary International. He lives in Big Spring with his wife, Susan. They have two sons and one grandson.